Villa
p. 39
Chris Llewellyn
see photo p. 14

Poets at Joaquin Miller's Cabin, 1984 - 2001

Joaquin Miller's cabin, which he built with a friend in the woods north of Washington, DC in 1883.

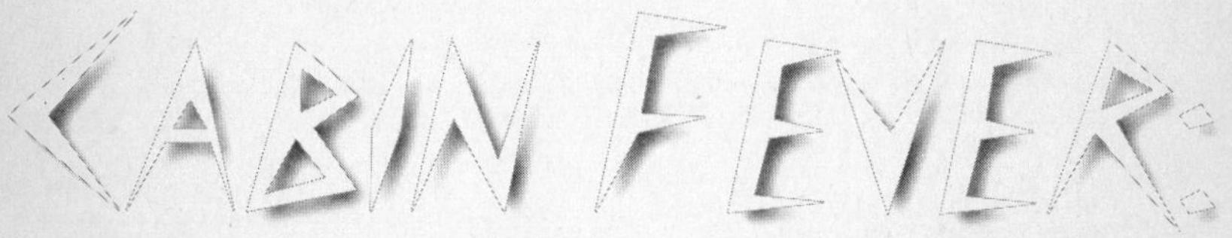

Poets at Joaquin Miller's Cabin, 1984 - 2001

Jacklyn W. Potter
Dwaine Rieves
Gary Stein

EDITORS

THE WORD WORKS
WASHINGTON, DC

First Edition
First Printing
Cabin Fever: Poets at Joaquin Miller's Cabin, 1984 - 2001

THE WORD WORKS gratefully acknowledges grants from the D.C. Commission on the Arts and Humanities, the long-standing cooperation of the National Park Service, the support from our contributors, and the donated services by the talented individuals that made this publication possible.

Book design, typography by Janice Olson
Cover art: Janice Olson

Library of Congress Control Number: 2002107014
International Standard Book Number: 0-915380-51-X

In Memoriam

Agha Shahid Ali

Roland Flint

Karlis Freivalds

Betty Parry

Garth Tate

Reetika Vazirani

Joaquin Miller, 1837-1913

Dedicated to Joy, Cathy, and in memory of Marjory Innes

Contents

All quotes above are from Joaquin Miller's poem, "Isles of the Amazons, Prelude," a selection from his book, *Songs of the Sun-Lands* (1873).

Poetry Under The Stars

The stars are in your hands. This anthology offers you work of the poets who read their poetry under the stars, next to Joaquin Miller's Cabin in Rock Creek Park, Washington, D.C., from 1984-2001. Established in 1975 by The Word Works, the Joaquin Miller Cabin Poetry Series gained popularity, skillfully coordinated by Karren Alenier, President of The Word Works, a small press and literary organization. When Karren invited me to become director of these programs in 1983, I was delighted. In the fall of that year, The Word Works invited poets to read in celebration of the 100th anniversary of Miller building his log cabin just north of Washington City. Here Miller sought to write poetry and live close to nature.

Nevertheless, Joaquin Miller maintained an interest in national affairs, especially equal rights for all Americans. His views prompted President Cleveland to request that he become Superintendent of Indian Affairs in 1885. Miller declined the offer and moved to the Oakland Hills of California. There he built another cabin, an amphitheatre, planted more than 1,000 evergreens and eventually became known as "the poet of the Sierras." In keeping with Miller's love of nature, our poetry series features readings outside, next to his cabin, under the stars.

Reading poetry under the stars, in the woods, has called for certain arrangements. Necessary gear includes water for the poets, insect repellent for all, a portable table for materials, and plenty of series flyers (designed by Janice Olson). For audience seating we created a small amphitheatre, with the essential help of audience muscle-power, lugging several large picnic tables and locating them in a rough semicircle next to the Cabin. They faced tall trees, Rock Creek and the poets. For reserved seats, audience members would need to bring their own folding chairs or picnic blankets.

We provided a small microphone which, although important, was largely rejected by the poets in the 1980s. It was opening night in 1990, when many of the 80 poetry-lovers in the audience called out, "Louder! We can't hear you!" to poets Beth Joselow and John Bradley. John and Beth were giving fine readings, but I knew we needed a better sound system. That week, I purchased a podium containing a battery-operated multi-directional microphone and speaker. This sound system purchase was fortunate, for the final reading in 1990 featured Lucille Clifton with Young Poets Competition winners Sarah DeWeerdt and Melissa Levine reading to an audience of 140 and, for their "Literary Visions" program, National Public Television filmed the reading under the stars.

The Miller Cabin Poetry Series has established traditions. Readings are always on Tuesday evenings. For years, on opening night, Robert Sargent has begun the series reading Miller's poem, "Columbus." With Bob, the audience sometimes repeats Miller's refrain: "Sail on! And on!" At every reading a guest book has been circulated, in part to show the need for a Park Service grounds permit. The Word Works has long been committed to paying the poets for their readings. In annual fund-raising efforts, The Batir Foundation and many private contributors have enabled us to keep that commitment, and to cover the other costs of the Series. Each year, many have also given their time and talent to bring poets to the cabin.

Another tradition grew from the effort to publicize these programs. In the late 1980s, The Word Works requested permission from the National Capital Region to place a durable sign in front of the cabin announcing the readings. Going through the administrative channels, permission was obtained and an attractive sign was built next to the cabin and Park path by Robert Lindsey. Complete with plexiglas, lock and cedar-shake roof, it was large enough to display the year's series flyer and a photograph of each poet. How fortunate for us to have Lori Day become our devoted Marquessa of the Marquee, as I called her, every week putting up new photos of poets who would read the following week! Sign readers—walkers, joggers, cyclists—came, sometimes to their first poetry reading. One day in the 1990s, Lori went down to post photos, but could not find the sign. It had finally succumbed to natural forces: rain, snow and creatures of the woods. The Park's maintenance crew had removed its crumbled remains.

Summer rains have called for an alternative indoor site. The small cabin, over 100 years old, is best left for spiders and other tiny creatures of nature. My house on Kennedy Street, just five minutes from the cabin, became the Miller's Cabin "East Wing," an arrangement completely supported by Marchant (Lucky) Wentworth, poetry-lover and owner of the old house, who always helped to drag out old chairs, set up the sound system, and turn on the vent fan on warm D.C. summer nights. Following every reading, rain or shine, I have encouraged everyone at the cabin to celebrate the poets by coming to my home for a reception with wine, refreshments, and good conversation. Our receptions have featured classical guitarist Michael Davis since the 1990s.

A special tradition has been the annual readings, since 1988, by winners of The Word Works Young Poets Competition. This program has presented two high-school age poets and an established poet honoring these winners. First coordinated by Gail Collins-Ranadive, this reading has featured the young poets with Lucille Clifton, Michael Collier, Roland Flint, Rod Jellema, E. Ethelbert Miller, Faye Moskowitz, Stanley Plumly, Reed Whittemore and many more (See Page 208, "The Word Works Young Poets Competition Winners.") In their readings, these experienced writers speak to the young poets, directly and in their poems. One young poet exclaimed, "This is the happiest day of my life!" The Young Poets Competition continues now under the lively leadership of Perry Epes.

Like stars, the poets here wink and sparkle in their diversity. Living in Washington, D.C., the city of embassies, travelers worldwide, and Congressional representatives, I have been determined to find and present good poets from not only the U.S. but also from other countries. Foreign or American, this anthology includes, for example, poets Moshe Dor, Guang-Shing Cheng, Vladimir Levchev, Sydney March, Lyubomir Nikolov, Alicia Partnoy, Luis Rebaza-Soraluz, May Rihani, Martha Sanchez-Lowery, Shan Shi, Askold Skalsky and Hilary Tham, among others. These poets read their marvelous work in their native language and in English, sometimes reading with their translators.

One evening at the cabin, a man from the audience named Robert Darling came to me and said he had a connection to Joaquin Miller. In the late 1880s, Isabel Darling, his ancestor, traveled with her husband to California's Oakland Hills. She quickly became friends with a neighbor.

"Joaquin Miller!" I exclaimed.

Robert nodded, telling me that Isabel was also a poet. He continued, "She owned something Miller was quite interested in. Can you guess what it was?" I couldn't.

Robert Darling smiled and said, "A typewriter. She typed many of his poems, which surely helped him get published. It seems he was often in the right place at the right time."

This anthology would not be in your hands if I had not had the privilege of working with Dwaine Rieves and Gary Stein. Their superb work shines on every page. We thank the completely supportive members of The Word Works—Karren Alenier, Hilary Tham, Robert Sargent, Michael Davis, Dr. Jim Beall, Janice Olson, and others on the staff, who have made all the difference.

May the poetry in this anthology give you peace and pleasure. If you've been to Joaquin Miller's Cabin to hear the poets, may the memories return. Join the poets now, under the stars. It's the right place! It's the right time!

Toujours le mot,

Jacklyn W. Potter
Director

I

"WHERE THE DARK PINES TALK"

—Joaquin Miller

POETS READING 1984-1989

and the 1983 Cabin construction centennial reading

CONTENTS

ABOVE: Miller Cabin Poetry Series director Jacklyn Potter and Karren Alenier, the Series' founder, in 1989.

RIGHT: Anne Becker reads while Ivan Alenier holds the mike at the 1983 cabin construction centennial reading.

FACING PAGE: Shirley Cochrane reads in 1984, TOP. Michael Hauptschein, Miller Cabin's hardy perennial and unofficial photographer, hangs his signatory banner in 1986, BELOW.

PREVIOUS PAGE: Jacklyn Potter giving one of her scintillating introductions in 1984, TOP. The sturdy marquee, with photos of Sunil Freeman and Fareedah Allah, 1988, BELOW.

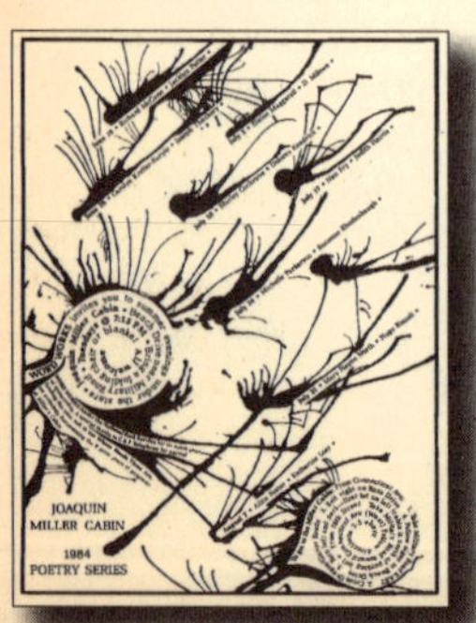

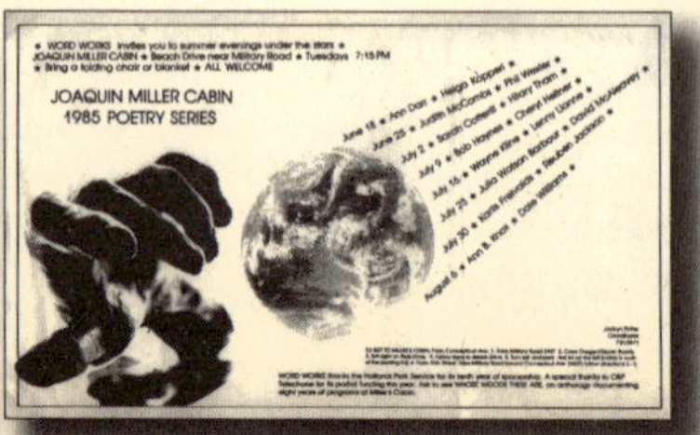

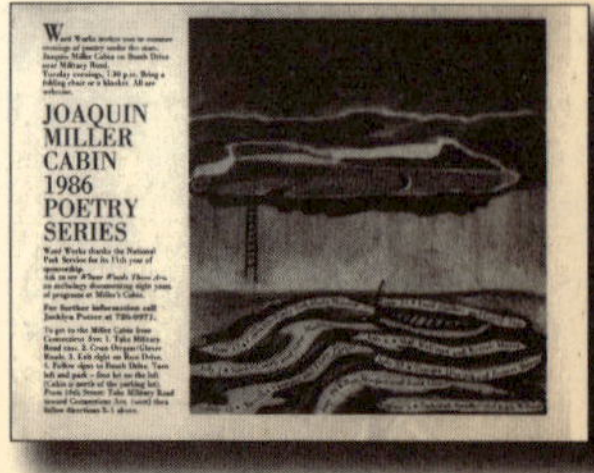

DARK PINES - - -

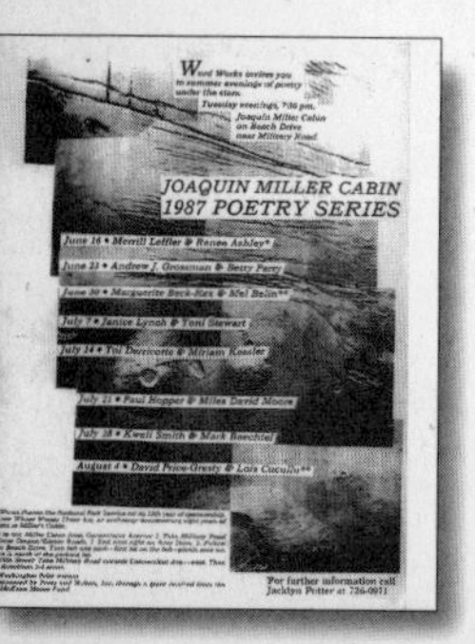
JOAQUIN MILLER CABIN
1987 POETRY SERIES
For further information call
Jacklyn Potter at 726-0971

ABOVE LEFT, FROM THE TOP: Christopher Bursk, 1988 Washington Prize winner; Chris Llewellyn, 1989; and Robin Suleiman, first Young Poet winner, 1988, read at Jacklyn's house, Kennedy Street, rainy-day location.

ABOVE, RIGHT: Robert Sargent, the Godfather of Washington Poetry, reads Joaquin Miller's "Columbus" to open 1988 Series.

RIGHT: Poetry can sometimes tickle you, as it does poets Roland Flint and Betty Parry, here in 1988.

Roland Flint

The Green for Pamela

After she had witnessed and somehow survived her twin brother's death, my daughter Pamela and I would lie across the bed, staring out the window at dusk, and see what human faces and animal shapes we could see or make in the waving green tops of the darkening trees.

When the streetlights came on, it was different, and beautiful still: the leaves, resuming green, were on our side of the lamp, the light lighting the tree and shining through to us, like daytime—cleaner, though, and greener.

But it was best just before the lights came on: we would be there and talk and wait for a little dark and a little wind to make the trees move and sough and whisper as they rearranged the human faces and animal shapes of night—an elephant nodding, a dog wagging or leaping, Mr. Bishop's face in Mr. Bishop's tree.

It's been three years and I don't remember now if I knew those nights I was leaving, I don't think so. But we had already left the happy shouting, the dancing, wrestling and marching games before bed.

And we were looking for a quiet way to translate night into the green human faces and animal shapes we knew to move in the sun all day and to wait all night for our return, resuming green.

Nan Fry

Hickory Bed

I want to make a poem big
as a bed, a poem to hold
us while we sleep,
with the moon rising over
our heads and sunlight
warming our feet, a poem made
from slow-growing hickory,

with a long taproot
and husks that burst
when they're ripe,
a poem that claims
the forest at climax,
that drinks the light
and knows the dark,
a poem sanded smooth to the touch,
with an open grain and sweat
in its creases, a poem that molds
itself to our bodies.

Philip Wexler

The Calculus of Ants on a Worm

Swarming tiny
bodies nibble
away, no limits,

at the squirming
tube, divide,
reduce

by degrees,
make of it
null,

nothing original
this derivative
devouring,

flitter around
the tail end
of the curve,

march off,
a tight triangle,
bellies full,

infinite,
temporary
satisfaction,

leave behind
the stain
of an integral sign.

Paul Grant

Stand-up Daffodils

Somebody Sky King's age at least
clatters a dragonfly toward the municipal
airport. In the roadside yards beginning to turn
green and give themselves over to dandelions,
trailers sprout signs in hopes of selling
the johnboats of the dead.

A grouse that flew its buckshot burden
as far as it could and fell in my driveway
I've bagged and buried, and its loose pinfeathers
have blown away in the same wet wind
that blew these blossoms down on broken stalks
to justify my cutting them for keeps,

but now it's dropped to a breeze that likes to pretend
it played piano in a cathouse in Biloxi,
Mississippi when it was young,
and it's trying to get under my shirt and feel
around for my heart, that dirty joke
whose punch line I'd forgotten.

Robert Haynes

Peonies

for Jacklyn Potter

This is not about all those elegies
we read to autopsies and body parts
made lovely with images of spring

nor about cassettes we played
over and over for a clarity
gained only later with wine.

This is not about stars dying
in Joe's strophes to supernovas,
although I liked your comment

about how the saddest are small
White Dwarves who disappear
without fanfare. You nearly cried

at how they fade as molecules
fuse to heavier elements, until
their light simply goes out—leaving

no guidepost over Bethlehem, no
remarkable corpse. This is not
an illumination of prophecies,

nor a speech aimed straight
as the stamen on lilies. This is only
about peonies with tiny feet

of ants plying bulbs, trailing parades
to a box sitting cockeyed on a chair.
This is about a quintrillion ants

looking at papers and paperclips
for anything potable—it's about
how some will die in that box; some

will hunker themselves in the dark
corners of cardboard, growing
drunk and starry-eyed on talking.

Suzanne Rhodenbaugh

When That Sweet Wind Through My Southern Window Comes

I like to trace where it's been, the half moon curve of sweep
begun just west into Alabama, I imagine, and come across
some low-slung parts of Florida, Georgia, the Carolinas.

To reach Virginia it's crossed the Chattahoochee, the Sewanee,
the Savannah, gone over the Cape Fear River and the Tar
and passed, close by here, our river linked forever

to lost causes and surrender: Appomattox. I guess it's blown
dangerous and lovely in gusts and wisps across
Confederate dead and kudzu and moon vines,

and long distance rigs hauling computer junk so we can have
more of nothing faster. And military installations
we'd rather not know about and malls and the mud,

still, and the lightning bugs: the whole shebang, really,
all the mess: the chickens murdered for our delight, the hogs
butchered on our behalf Jesus there's no end to the eating.

So, like I say, when that sweet wind comes up and strokes
the drift of my aging jawline, and causes the bedclothes
to rise, just for a moment, with the added ghosts,

well, it's just gentle and cool and consoling
as the child I'd like to believe I once was
in the time I'd like to believe I once had.

Jacklyn W. Potter

Boundaries

That wildflower name
you called me   shatters
    to kaleidoscope
fall   you fly like pollen

but I am
as composed   as a daisy
tight   as a green
fig's hold   I am wound

regular as rope   a kitchen
timer ticking   a cold oven   waiting

while the small   bright suns   in the field
        transform   themselves

Light   had been everywhere
        until my hands
            covered the sun

Sarah Cotterill

You Filed in the Oldest Paths

that followed the rise,
past woodlot and combine

graveyard, lime pit and slough

we considered the weight of what you gave
freely:

more than we could ever use ran, raw
into the pail

DARK PINES -

fashioned of ditch water and trace
minerals that
changed in us, becoming

rib and femur, brain pan and pelvis

draught that could mute
panic, call
sleep, halter
loss   of bone

white stream meant for the calf

succor

whole ration you made
out of the very grass

Cheryl Hellner

Wind-bound

1.
Tattered threads
of rain and storm light.
Wind-bound
cold
you wait on an island.

2.
Even if you are frightened. Even if you are without comfort
you can stand
still in the rain and wonder
at its long journey
from sea to air to your own skin
to the pale tips of your fingers.

3.
After the pins of lightning
After the gray rags of thunder—
Whose cry passed
like a golden cord
through the wind's blue eye?

And whose prayer lifted the latch
flung wide the body's
iron door?

4.
And when you stepped out from beneath
the spruce and fir trees and felt
this sun-woven shawl, the sudden warmth, this rippling
pleasure
Did you not glimpse the loon—that dark and plaintive traveler—
gliding out from the narrow cove onto the open water?

And did you not see her head flung back?
And did you not hear her
singing

James McEuen

The Debt

Wind called from the moon's
black throat, out full
copper lips, and I answered
(I was sixteen; it was midnight),
prayed into it, to the Devil.
By names that came right to mind—
foolish babble, of course,
adolescent melodrama. Why I've
even forgotten what I asked for,
so little seems to have come of it,
as little as comes from God.

DARK PINES -

But how strange in this warm dark
to wake thinking of that...

The window rattles again
with a braying wind off the mountains,
and my good wife stirs with the sound,
my wife who dreams of babies. Outside
the window you can't tell
frost from moonlight on the coiled
waste of the garden, that looks trampled
by some cloven hooves, so barren—
and my nape hair bristles
at the wind like a hand
on the sash: *The debt,*
the debt. O God,
what
did I promise!

Kermit Moyer

The Dream of Return

Running down a narrow path, in the woods
in back of the cabin, ducking the tickle
of spider webs, deeper into the dark, I

evade the reach of sucker vines and drop
to the ground, my arms shielding my head:
roll under the perfumed skirt of a spruce

to my hide-out's cushioned floor: lie there
suspended, catching my breath, then sit cross
legged and still: count time by the stitches

the fireflies make in this feathery screen
of fir: wait until everyone's caught but me
and there's no one else left who can save them.

-1984-1989

Mel Belin

Webs

Like wisps of morning fog
not burnt off, or festive
bunting on buttonbush,
lizard's tail. An odd patchwork
of directions in these spider
webs: slanted diagonal
vertical athwart in
meadow wetlands. We, who
have been stuck, hand here,
heart there, weave our lives beside
the like of these, spinning out
the fabric too, sometimes
invisible, not sure
if any of it can be
undone. Salvador Dali—
his limp clocks folded over
branches like slices
of cheese or linen to dry—
would've loved to paint all
of this. He, who understood
the timelessness in perfervid
phenomena, would've reached
for his palette, but now
instead of blood and maggot,
the fine silken strand.

Karren L. Alenier

Something Growing

Viscous as honey, sweet
as the dew of that suckle
weed: honey, oh, honey! my

DARK PINES -

petals burn when you plant
yours on mine.
It's agriculture
without politicians in smoke-
filled caucus rooms.
Zeus
catapults those bolts of
lightning. Can you catch
that as I nab the electrical
charge from you?
Rain, rain,
rain and then the sun paints
us green not envy not.
Look
at the roots and the air-
born stalks feeling
their way.

Elaine Magarrell

White Butterflies

I have always loved
fireflies. And a wide variety
of faces. And going
away—the fine view of rivers

from the plane. The first fish
I ever caught was big. We fried
and ate it although I was never
to catch another. Even knowing this
I would not have framed it.

My first romantic kiss
was cold and slimy. My mind
broke once. That was when I thought
of how the sea cannot stop itself.
The sun does not shine
willingly. The owl may decide

to bring death to the mouse but cannot
decide against its own living.

I step into the garden to watch
the white butterflies flicker
on and off around
the pincushion flowers
the way, at times,
I watch my life
as if it were not mine
to end or save.

Jean Johnson

Morels

Like sex, morels require fire.
Out of the ash under pine poles
stripped naked by last year's fire,
on duff black as hell's terrain
they appear.

Netted like tripe on the butcher's slab
Devil's thumbs, soot-colored,
they push up from the muck,
an almost invisible treasure
luring men.

In a meadow dealers set up tents:
"Mushrooms bought."
"Nine dollars a pound."
"They go for forty-five in New York."
"The airport handles twenty thousand pounds in season."

This is season. We had come to pay respects
to river milky with spring run-off
to mountains frosted with yesterday's snow
perhaps to moose or bear.
Instead we find along the North Fork Road campers,

vans, pick-ups and people sooty as miners hunting
in scorched forest
where nothing is growing
but these children of disaster
Devil's offspring, delicious as sin.

Thomas M. Kirlin

Why the Soul Loves Catfish

Let's just say an elegant man
in a loose blue nightcap

with nothing on his mind
but the sky, surprised us

tracking game by starlight,
shot you in the blind,

made off with the lamps of madness
& climbed, scattering as ransom

this palpable absence
only time can refine—

swirling her honey head, making
our bed, as constant as taxes

& crime...Welcome, if you can
girls & boys, an old roommate of mine

a son-of-a-gun, a hell of a guy,
a cat whose ass rattles buckshot:

the warden, my soul,
serving life, plus 99.

Doris Brody

Place of the Turtles Bay

The night no turtles came ashore
we walked miles on the damp
sand at the water's edge
looking into gray upon gray
for dark shapes rowing
out of the waves. We waited
beside the ocean, warm
and breathing, lit only by stars
blazing in the moonless sky,
saw first one then another
streak into nothing.

We waited, our voices hushed,
and silence slipped into us.

The recent days—a riptide
of rocks, screeches, scowls—
spilled out like a bad movie,
the focus fuzzy, the sound missing.
The constellations inched westward,
and the arms of the scorpion
began to reach for the path
the sun took into the trees.

We will find a place to put those days,
into a moonless night without turtles,
into a sky leaking stars.

Michael C. Davis

Hunger

The old heron in the river
takes one stitch a day,
one stitch...

DARK PINES --

basting the water's edge
to the shade overhanging the bank.

Leg-deep in a seam
of hydrilla, his patience
seems infinite. He stands
over his piece of river
like a cloud,
his prey drawn to its shelter.

Everything is searching,
and the night will be long.

A quick stab,
and he is fed.

At dusk, he flies,
unlabored,
each wing beat sure,
over the fabric of homes
knit shoulder to shoulder,
where we sleep
as close together
as our hungers will allow.

Over us all he coils,
a single letter without a word.

Elaine Magarrell

Looking up from the Garden

Even in sun
after last night's
storm, even
with three kinds of roses
in full bloom—
house and bodies are
quietly falling

apart. Grout squeezed
from between
the bricks. Flesh dropping
from arm bones
like flashing
slumped from the wall.

Words slow to come.
Doors that will not close.
Pillars of dust. Faucets
forever on
like fountains
at a gravesite.
One day the curious

will invade these ruins
where we'll lie mummified,
carvings of birds like dogs
at our feet—
their shrimp-fork toes
aloft. There will be

a memento shop
to see replicas
of my cooking pots,
your recipe for wild tea.
Guides will raise
their umbrellas.

Here.
Over here.
This is where
people were happy.

DARK PINES -

Mark Baechtel

The Roasted Swan Sings

after the Carmina Burana

The arrow in its flight
becomes the turning spit;
the axis of the world
if we but thought of it.

Lenny Lianne

Nocturne

The curtains billow and go flat,
and billow again.
Her hand reaches out and finds
the empty side of the bed.
Outside the open door
the water trembles silver.
Here the boats, dark shadows,
are content in their moorings.

Forget the darkness, she says;
the stars, you know,
shine whether you try
to touch them or not.

Distant music sifts in and out,
like accidental angels crooning
that the body insists on dreams,
a flotilla of images
to whisper everything
sacred is remembered.

Hilary Tham

Standing in the dark, seeing Orion's Belt

listening to American frogs say "Ribbit, Bud - weiser,"
I ask myself: What if poets did not write
about death?
Would poems be forgotten
as helium balloons
that delight us a span and rise,
stringless, into sky?
Would we miss the stars, stars whose names
recall dead civilizations and their gods?

What if death did not exist? Would we
treasure the wisdom of the Greeks if they
were not ancient, merely old? Would we
take a trial subscription to their monthly journal?
Those Greek sagas make juicier reading than
the National Inquirer!

Would we need to make decisions?
Or commitments?
                    Shall I smell a rose?
Or write prose? Who will read it
when it's published?
                              Will publishers
take real instead of virtual centuries
to get that book into print?

Would we take our time, a decade or ten,
to reach a decision, another eon
to reconsider and reach another?
Would we smash our clocks, pause a hundred years
to contemplate a tree or a dog's bark?

I want to praise the breakable heart, biological
clock that makes us run, trying to beat the dark.

Judith McCombs

Pictures Not in Our Albums

Somewhere it is still
a dream of safety, our young
parents hauling us up the dark pass,

Father blocking the wheels of the trailer
while Mother lets go the emergency brake
and eases the Ford into low, pulls forward
and slows, pulls forward and waits.
As if I had watched from a roadcut

I see the small oval Ford
pale in the shadows, our grey-blue trailer
weighing it down, the asphalt road
falling away on all sides into blackness,
the curve ahead climbing to blackness.

Across the vast basin of desert,
the night-drowned ridges and foothills,
a coyote howls and is answered. There are
no lights but ours on the earth,
no farther lights except the slow stars.

In the back of the car, in the warm
nest of children, I drift
from sleep to waking, breath
to breath, as the car labors
and rests, labors and rests,

and the night outside is a slow swelling sea
lapping the mountains, black waters
so vast that a ship could founder,
a thousand lit ships go down,
all lights but our own go under.

Fareedah Allah

Great Googa Mooga

The Cadillac with the North Star system
Stole my Santa Claus.
My big fine man, my dog, my baby boo
Drove up in a red & white silver Eldorado,
Grinning from ear to ear, telling me that
We were driving to North Carolina to see his mama.
I wanted to scream, jump up&down
What about my mink coat? My FUBU sweatsuit?
Have you lost your mind? Who in the Hell said I wanted
To see your mama? He was standing there smiling, waving
At the neighbors.
My Boo drove up in a brand new Cadillac with the
North Star system. He had a big red bow tied on the hood
And a big grin on his face: "Merry Christmas, Babygirl!"
"Happy New Year to you!"
That Cadillac with the North Star system stole my Santa Claus:
My hoochie mama designer's dress, my sock-it-to-you three-inch heels from
    Payless,
And my cell phone. Goddamn!! General Motors, carjacked my Christmas!
I got duel airbags, anti-lock brakes, a V8 motor that can go from 0 - 60 mph
In less than a minute.
I am waving goodbye to Santa Claus, my new hair, my nails, that Gucci bag
I put on Lay-a-way. My man bought a red&silver Eldorado.
So, we are driving to North Carolina to see his Soul Food cooking mama.
"Goddamn, General Motors!!!"

Judith McCombs

Afterwards, You Learn

Afterwards, you learn to say
you were lucky, the last-year's cubs
stayed safely behind her, breaking
the thickets for berries. Lucky
the wind from the darkening valley

DARK PINES -

turned cold, and your jacket was heavy,
and zipped to the neck. Lucky
you knew, too late for retreat
in that clearing of downfall and stone,
to drop and go fetal, arm
over neck, playing dead. Lucky
the backpack came off like an arm,
saving most of your arm, and kept her
busy till the grunting cubs
called her back to their feast.

Afterwards you learn to say
that the fault was yours: you were tired,
you were stubborn, making up for lost time
on that summer-growth trail through clearings
and thickets, the wind in your face,
not bothering to sing out or warn
what was there besides you, not waiting
for warnings to reach you.

But sometimes, in sleep, you go back
to that stonefall clearing, that edge
of safety where your scalp hair rises
like hackles for no reason you see,
and there is still enough time to go back
as that dark shape lifts upright
from its tangle of shadow, like a man
in a burly fur suit, peering out,
and you wake with the ghost hairs rising
like fur on your unscarred neck
and perfect right arm.

Howard Gofreed

Lave

I float on my back in my parents'
bathtub in a scum of soap
and my own dead skin, staring

at the wide uneven band of aging
original caulk that says
this tub never stood flat on the floor,

staring past the missing piece
below the faucet, eye to eye
with a beady roach behind the wall

of pink tiles bulging with hidden urges,
old hidden urges, so many it sags
down and over the tub's edge

and does not meet flush with the other
wall, full of its own passions, the line
of their joint not straight but a crooked

fall to caulk and tub, and I wonder
why, when a child, I did not see
the crazy angles of this house.

Kim Roberts

As in a Fable

Clapboard painted white
and glowing in the sunlight:
                                        the vertical lines

of the white exterior staircase
                                        ascend, and its shadow,
purpled and wavering, ascends
in tandem. These lines,
                                where brightness stuns,
suggest one language.

The shadow-stair
                follows, as meaning follows
words, rippling

in and out of focus, and just
one step behind. You pass
this house daily,

have passed a thousand times
without hearing its thrumming alto,
low and steady, vibrating
at your exact frequency.

Your house, further down the block,
lies waiting. But this one
has stopped you.
Its shape is subsuming into yours.

That ruffled shadow makes the white
stand out blindingly pure:
the absence of color

like the saintly mirage
that appears in the midst of the desert,
or the blinding tunnel
the dead are said to walk toward.

Mary Ann Daly

The Hard Life of the Upstairs People

Late-night Wednesday between twelve and one
the upstairs people start to rearrange
their furniture, dragging divan
to dining room, rolling up the rug.
By two they're ready for the race.
Up the front steps and across the porch they chug,
unlock the front door, slam the screen,
slam the door, rush to the back, unlock
the back door, slam it and the screen,
run down the back stairs as if to attack
the dog next door, and up again

to the dog's cheers, and out the front and back
and forth until, by three or four,
they seem to lose the spirit of the game,
having already lost track of the score.
Exhausted, they fling their rocking chairs upon
the wooden floor and creak themselves
to a hard-earned sleep, sometime around dawn.

Robin Suleiman

The Vendor

The Vendor was waiting,
he had seen the girl at the gate,
one arm ribboned in
setting sun.
I know what you need,
and his voice was like wind
over stones.
The girl drank the sound
and still thirsted.
She wondered why father had warned,
why the Vendor
still held space in this yard,
his smooth tongue
sliding in like a knife
slicing off days
and present places,
the girl drinking truth
from his basket of lies.

The Vendor said Try,
stroked her hair,
said I know,
and he did,
with night crouching silent behind him.
The fruit burst
fell from its stem

DARK PINES -

in a rush like the blood
and the Vendor said, Taste,
but bite deep.
With the fresh-fallen,
the bitterness lies close to the skin.

Chris Llewellyn

Villa

No more housework or lazy delays.
Unplug the tube, let laundry go rot.
I gotta compose a sonnet today.

Before my Friday's frittered away
forget this dust, that greazy pot.
No more housework or lazy delays.

Writing in form is better than pay
or made up beds or floors new mopt.
I gotta compose a sonnet today.

No fixing a salad or fried fish feelay,
grooming the pooch or stopping to shop.
No more housework or lazy delays.

Hide in the bedroom or if I can't stay
go skulk in the cellar under a lock.
I gotta compose a sonnet today.

Move over Wordsworth, Milton, Millay.
Skillet stay cool, my fourteener is hot!
No more housework or lazy delay.
I'm gonna compose a sonnet today.

--1984-1989

Christopher Bursk

A Very Short Sonnet Cycle

1

Away with thee, self-loving lads whom Cupid's arrow
never glads. So is this about masturbation?
I remember asking my tenth grade teacher.
The only way I could tolerate sonnets was to turn them
dirty. All that posturing. So many gripes, moans, sighs
all those breaths expended on a pretty face,
all those pretty speeches
as if the poet's doing his best to turn the beloved into nothing
but air, pull him down
into the lungs, translate him
into blood and hoard the beauty there.
And so in nets of vanity lie taken.
All those labors to look easy, the deep sincerity
of all those dissemblings, the contrivances of passion.

2

Sir Philip Sidney, expiring, called only for a sip
of wine, and then, before he could drink,
yielded the cup to a common soldier, who,
as his biographer, Fulke Greville, put it,
had eaten his last at the same feast,
one dying man holding a cup to another dying man's lips
and saying only *Thy necessity is greater than mine.*
Fulke Greville himself, after being stabbed,
gave strict instructions that his fleeing assailant not be pursued,
desiring that *Not any man should lose his life*
for me. At fifteen I'd trouble understanding that
it's not only the gesture, not just what we've done,
that matters, but how we speak of it
that proves our mettle, as if that's all we'll be left,
these words, their hard choices.

Susan Sonde

As Participants in a Major Production in a Classical Mode

We have been sticking out our necks
long enough, ears too,
pressed against the existential maw
of a universe which does not hear us,
and hides behind the exuberance of omission.

The choice of players, the banners,
their festive colors were up to us
the wins and losses though, were not,
nor could they be
counted on to make us happy;
if we knew what that happiness was,
if the others also knew and would tell us.

As for the unfinished quality of our lives,
the speculative tacked on at the end was over;
the theater in the round; the money, the worry
beads designed to get us through these times.
The material plays to a packed house and no one,
absolutely no one, shows the slightest interest
in something which has taken so much
of our time, that fidgets and demands
and promises so little.

While the Director, the One wearing the cap
with visor that makes Him invisible
speaks into the megaphone,
makes his coarse jokes, His bid
for some way into our conversation.

Carolyn Kreiter-Foronda

On Monet's Studio-Boat

From his studio-boat I can see better: morning
haze, its ghostly vapor leaping
into the river's mouth, plum-cloaked and opening.

Beneath first light: ripples flooding,
sea pearls, pink and swelling.
I can see better from the studio-boat: morning

sweeping down: gulls gliding
over glassy surface, wing-shadows floating
into the river's mouth, wind-soaked and opening.

The suddenness of anything: a passing
locomotive, its blue fumes parting.
I can see better from the studio-boat: morning's

masterwork: orchid winging
across sky. Maker of water diving
into the river's mouth, lavender and opening.

Luffs of sails billowing, the day soaring.
A violin, the sun arrives, trilling.
From the studio-boat I can see better: morning
rises out of the river's mouth, wine-gold opening.

Shirley Cochrane

View as Art

Observe the impressionist painting made
by the slanted maple with red-wine pods
soon to be transformed into day-glo leaves
and behind this tree, the washed blue sky
bisected randomly by a stripe of cloud.
At midpoint the giant blossoming pear
is blown by hefty March winds which also
rearrange clouds and supple maple boughs.

DARK PINES - - -

But as we watch this ever-moving art
we can see, imposed upon pear tree
(corner, left), the roof and chimney
of a neighboring house that anchor
the painting in space and hold it fast
as March gives way to April, April
to May, and through the calendar year—
this street, this city, these lives...

Enid Shomer

In The Viennese Style

In the Cafe Imperial, they are bringing out
the Mozart cake with its delicate

pistachio creme. I've been watching the linden
leaves as the wind lifts them

into the streetlights, how they blanch, then darken
as if they are having an argument

with the tree. On the Ringstrasse, trams
wheeze past and lines of home-

bound traffic blur to faint septic streaks.
The scrolls and curves of the Baroque—

lush, gold-leafed, excessive—look like nothing now
to me but hearts stretched out

of shape, the way tonight the soloist
took music plucked on strings and twisted it

through brass. We had a happy week in perhaps
the only city where we could feel

our marriage healed when actually it was forsaken,
utterly lost, when actually it came

to this: we could agree on what was beautiful,
that was all.

Sibbie O'Sullivan

Suburbia

Outside Magoo's,
beneath a muraled wall of Dublin,
across the street from the Vietnamese nail salon,
we are eating pizza in almost moonlight.
An angel floats by on wings made out of paper towels
and sings to us, "Tonight's special..."
with lips as scarlet as the scarlet sky.

Meanwhile in some other 'burb,
"The gunman freed 10 hostages in exchange for 3 sixpacks of Bud,"
and in another, "Hundreds report seeing the Virgin Mary
appear above the bean fields."
Here it's more salt, more napkins,
and for our fairy tale the Little Tavern's neon gingerbread.

Nietzsche says you must make friends again with the nearest
things.
To what, then, shall we make a toast?
To the cars sliding past, lanterned from below like creatures
from the sea,
to the Lycra girls who strut by on cigarettes, their toes aflame,
bags of carryout swinging at their knees.

We lift our glasses to the boring beauty of the world,
to honeysuckle's sweet libido,
the cop's blared nipple bleeding out across the parking lot.

To see one thing one time, however small or dirty.
To Heaven, then,
its pulse, its shimmer, its golden arches.

Wayne Kline

Cat Paws for Delilah

"This is where his Creole brother landed," she said. "I was thanking you for saving my popcorn and I just thought of that." A coy beetle attacked his nose, crimson and flaring. "The government wants us to think it's the government, but it's not." The government wants us to think that coral fishermen want us dead, then they want us to wear clothes of a certain cut and ride in Harumba Vans with towels and little elastic comet-oids firing at us."

I was too ashamed to barter for lentils. I had misguided the market, and Polly was wrenching for a closet-shop on the East Side while Terry searched for her Visa. The time to rise up was not now, but from one room to the other the walls ceased dividing. Antsy Dave drew the barium through his lips, his careless spittle pooling sock-like at his naked feet.

"Whose shared belongings were never mine." Like reading his tabloid to a wiener in the fridge, while burglars undid the panty drawer. The shock of waking up under all that underwear, his taxonomic disciples sharpening their hindquarters. "I thought of myself one winter, 'n the freeze, and these sled dogs always hung around, harnessed to some kind of bladed contraption."

"God was sinking those ships for us, smashing our enemies' balls."
"God was sinking those balls for us, smashing our enemies' ships."
The pantheon shelling continued until the summer catalog expired. When the fall catalog arrived, shelling resumed, in sector four and along the only road leading out. "Four different Jeffcoat prisoners were exchanged for a bending Thumbelina rehearsal chart, and a brass fixture."

I was thinking I was paid to. This very good blending of window-shopping and country western whiskers shorn and shaken, the hairiest martini. "Why's a cowboy like that?" she asked. "The times we visited the campsites, they looked all sleepy. Or offended."

-1984-1989

David McAleavey

February: Arlington

Apparently the house produces them, like dust bunnies or drips in the sink taps, these kindergarten valentines, and they litter countertops, tables, and floors, insistent effusions of I LOVE YOU MOMMY or I LOVE YOU DADDY, sentiments not always evident in the squabbling dailiness of teeth, hands, hair, clothes, food, books, toys, space, and time. They appear always genuine, even when boast or propitiation, even when only technical exercises, shapes or colors to be admired, glue-work or staple-and-tape-work or freehand-drawing-work not previously attempted that way, or words formed neatly or swervingly around the complex curves of the heart. All acts of love, maybe, are this way, genuine even when self-serving or short-sighted, hyphenated-and-qualified, and like the valentines left here and there, sometimes on purpose to be found, sometimes negligently abandoned, are both familiar and strange. So too, in the middle of winter, getting ready to merge with the rush streaming along the valley near Fort Myer, I looked up behind the Army fence to see a white parade stallion loping among maples, part of the scene and above it, of a different and childlike order, the order of valentines.

Michelle Parkerson

Hejira

Returning
smooth as mango
from the ruins of St. Pierre
I am armed for morning
I once forgot civilization
had time to decipher dreams

There
faces were tintypes:
hybrid
African
my own
The curious music

DARK PINES --

of colonized language
succumbs to Black lips
In Martinique
the world flowers

Returned
to these steel bones
traffic jams
I cling to postcards:
the last I saw of my reflection
the last of Zion's breath

Myra Sklarew

At the Syrian Border

Walking between two mine fields
I pretend I am a tourist here: What trees,
I say. What mountains. I mouth
slogans bitter as a salt sea.

The wind feeds on the basalt rock.
Under every eucalyptus there is
the yawning shadow of a bunker. My people
is an armed camp.

I remember a boy who made a bridge
of his body for the others to climb across.
They turned him into air and fire and earth.
And here is the place where a father

let his child down a knotted sheet
like Jacob, only not going up.
One child by one child down the ladder
of knots and when he himself climbed

down for the last time he found each one
murdered. O Jacob let us put away
our strange gods. My people is an armed
camp. Her sons wear old faces.

Deborah Wassertzug

Engraving Day

The trees were newly planted in the subdivision then,
and the little jail was new, next to the police station.
The house was next-to-new, that summer we moved in. We were
new Americans. We were learning the rules of owning.
And the first rules were: Make it yours. Mark it. Identify.
The police advised it, and so we did. On the morning

of the appointed day, my father gathered the machines
in the kitchen, and then powered up the electric pen
the police had loaned him. Large to small, he tattooed them all:
television, mixer, slide projector, tape recorder,
and so on, not forgetting to include the metronome—
as though a thief would consider swiping a thing that goes

tock-tock on the conscience. Tock-tock. Safe overrides sorry.
He lettered carefully, as though thorough marks prevented
loss. And the fact is, there has never been a broken lock,
no smash-and-grabs, and after thirty years, so few machines
have died, you could almost believe that early care gave them
courage to persevere, to gracefully accept repairs.

The day I coaxed my parents to remove their wedding rings,
I found writing inside each, in simple script. Date and names.

DARK PINES --

Lois Cucullu

Breathing Space

My mother never told me that having sex
the first time would be like getting
water up your nose—no wonder
her book, pushed to the back of the nightstand
drawer, that Patsy Rivet and I found
one afternoon and examined, huddled on the floor
between my parent's twin chenille spreads,
no wonder it said that women didn't peak
till their thirties. Whatever it meant,

that summer, Patsy and I, our bodies flat
as towels, watched the lifeguard on break
take practice dives at Audubon Park Pool,
jackknife, twist, double gainer, layout, swan—
it looked so easy—his body splitting
the surface, the water peeling like a zipper
all the way to the bottom, then he'd flip,
glide up, nostrils streaming. He never
used the ladder.

We lay there, the sun reddening the caps
of our shoulders, the new pink flesh
across the nose.

Reuben Jackson

love

after years
and years
of trying;
like drivers
all but pushing
our idle cars

back onto the
road,

the two of us—
older, survivors
of illness,
death,
the superficiality
of lattes,
will bump into
each other;
shoppers
on a quiet street
spilling nothing more
than canned goods,
nothing less than a
hello
reaching across the sidewalk
like a hand
which, without ceremony,
would hold yours,
as it would hold that slightly dented
can,
or the banister
leading to your
house.

Ann B. Knox

Circles

It is dangerous to break a round thing,
to disturb a circle. The foot must center
neat on a man-hole lid, the yellow crayon
keep within the sun. When my brother peeled
a golf ball and unwound the mile-long
rubber twine, he stopped before its center,
the poison core that gives the power to bound.

DARK PINES -

A life-saver grows thin as an old wedding-
ring and shatters to curved needles on the tongue.
It is dangerous to break a round thing,
but I disturbed the circle, burst out, wanting
something wild, something risky and I lied.

Our beers sweat rings on the table, the candle
throws a round of yellow light, you speak
of the children, of plans until I reach out
to draw a line between us. My finger slices
a wet circle, crosses the curved edge
of flickering light. You trace a coaster rim
but do not look at me, knowing it is dangerous
to break a round thing, to disturb a circle.

Sunil Freeman

Talking

Not quite poems but more
like the rind of poems,
how your wine glass, raised right,
coaxes a plump ruby from falling
afternoon light. How we know
the river scene, sun-dazed
shock of blue and white to silver,
could use a sailboat.
What the boaters might say.

I love it when you say "marinara,"
say anything at all, like
"try some of this."
A waft of butter and garlic
roams from your bowl to mine,
mine to yours, as our words
find a rhythm we might walk.
We look from the canvas
back to each other, touch glasses,
let the silence breathe a while,
then head on down that road.

Paul Hopper

*Chemical Attraction**

for Nancy Horton

It combines all the perfumes of Paris,
an exponential expression of the chestnut blossoms
in the Bois de Boulogne and the Bois de Vincennes.

It is the fifth distillation of sweetness,
making even the scales on their wings ache
as they rise to follow, swinging toward the source.

As they hurry toward her, they may moan in fear
at a pitch that strikes only the ears of bats
or of their converging fellow-flutterers.

They cluster in billions upon her tree
until the boughs break and the great trunk cracks
under their flaming passion's force.

* *"It has been soberly calculated that if a single female moth were to release all the bombykol in her sac in a single spray, all at once, she could theoretically attract a trillion males in the instant. This is, of course, not done."*

—Lewis Thomas, *Lives of a Cell*

Brian Gilmore

the godfather

(for adanya— 18 months)

that scene from the godfather which i have watched over and
over: the don has passed chasing his grandson through the vegetable
garden. the traitor has been revealed at the funeral: sad eyed abe vigoda.
abe vigoda asks the lawyer tom hayden to get him out for old times sake

DARK PINES -

because it was "just business." "can't do it sally," is all that is said. though abe is almost saved because of his face, that wonderfully precious, charitable face which could make a father cry because i am also a lawyer and this is what i see each night looking into my daughter's 18 month old eyes: abe vigoda. sad eyed, looking to be saved from the sandman.

now she is working on me and giving it her best shot with those despondent but hopeful abe vigoda eyes. my daughter has to sleep in her crib for trying to cut a secret deal with one of the other five new york families. she wants me to get her out for old times sake and she knows i am not strong and loyal like the lawyer tom hayden. i look into her eyes and replay that scene again. i see abe being led away to 'sleep with the fishes." francis ford coppola is lucky he didn't cast this 18 month old for his film. who would have believed that an infant black girl would one day run the mob.

Kwelismith

Totem

for Audre Lorde

When warrior woman refused
her normal ocean swim refused
her normal poem in the Sun

refused her abalone shell
My Lord What a Morning
a giant movement in black

remember the shaking
remember that tiedyeddress
this rainbow serpent wore

outside the renegade wisdom
of our dead behind us
walking under water

Remember the jolt
cracked fuchsia orange lightning
all at once a burst of

Lorde nightingale flapping
north her left wing dipping east
cut south fire knives shells and

bells lavender blue ribbon
poppies in copper hand
one shoe by any means

necessary Remember
eleanor bumper's shopping bag
flying one angel arm

Moon marked and touched by sun
meadow lark feathers in basket
Remember the roar

white communion shawl
blood satin sash
around her shoulders

We raised candles to light
this warrior home thousands
and thousands of candles

Myra Sklarew

Rosary

In braille you read the oval
shapes with your fingers They rise
in the earth necklace float
through red clay Call
the blue beads
to your fingertips They open
and climb toward you tendrils
of pain They glide their blue
bodies under the field One grows
there one of them clinging
to his wood

Renée Ashley

Obsolete Angel

This one can't fly: he's got
stubby wings, he's old
as space or time; he's gone
to fat. And now he even
disregards the omens that he never
should have learned to read
at all: blistered skies,
the sticky secrets
in the bowels of toads.
He's used up his store
of magic, he's half-blind,
but he's crusty
as good bread and willing:
in the moonlight,
he struggles up the shadows
towards god, hears
the wheezing orchestration
of embodied lives
—he always sings low,
his one hoarse note,
always tumbles down to where
we save him again
and again he falls
like a hailstone
from some heaven
and we will save him.

Enid Dame

Lot's Wife

I'm not surprised
this happened in some ways
I
was always numb

standing before the stove
braiding my daughters' hair

numb as a rock
in the ritual bath

hard to raise daughters
in that city
where men loved each other
or entertained angels

I always suspected
movement
was dangerous

they called him
the most righteous man
in Sodom in bed
I'd feel him
knocking against me
like someone opening
a window
in another room

now
I don't feel
anything at all.
It isn't so different.

Mary Hayne North

Woman Peeling Potatoes

for Sibylle Pearson

In the other room John is dying of AIDS
I slip another naked potato into the pot.
Outside the city could be Nevada
all I see these days is desert scrub unaware of my footsteps

DARK PINES --

unaware of the great monolith about to blast angrily underground.
The city doesn't seem to fucking care,
so I'm back working with "God's Love, We Deliver"
cooking potatoes for John who is homebound
is dying
while I burn like the center of the Earth
who knows creatures are setting firecrackers off
under her skin
as John knows.
I can't tell you how much I struggle to find meaning
just back from being arrested in a nuclear test zone.

Richard McCann

After You Died

I had a body again. And I could recall
how it had been, back then,

to want things. Easy to recall that now—
this sun-dazed room; lilacs, in white bowls.
But for a long time I was grateful
only for what your dying was taking from me:
the world, dismantling itself; soon there'd be no more obstinacies,
I wouldn't want anything again...

After you died I rode a bicycle around the lake all day, in circles.
I had come back. And so it was hard not to remember
how it had been walking the path that circled the lake
where I'd once gone each night to look for sex.
It's true that I drank heavenly

—*heavily*, I mean. I was drunk.
I walked until someone wanted me. But what did I hope
to love in return? —I followed him, his pale shirt disappearing
into a small clearing hidden by shrubs.
He undressed, his bare chest mottled by moonlight's shadows of leaves.
If I could have followed you like that, even in grief,

into a clearing littered with waded paper tissues
—white carnations!

Mostly I met no one.
The path ended by the public toilets.
I loitered by a row of urinals; or I stood outside,
beneath the dim, caged streetlamp,
in a body I hated. Without it,
who'd need to ask the world for a thing?

Hugo Rizzoli

Putting the Aerialists to Bed

The famous aerialists are packed in
for the night, leaving the high wire
to chance the obstacles of the hall;
a pair of slippers, a floor lamp, the edge
of an upturned carpet.

They have decided to go to bed,
to sleep through the night, breathing
rung to rung over their famous trapeze,
and fall asleep.

It is a night well spent, a swift
descent on the far side
of midnight. Who knows when
they'll be back this way again.

Karlis Freivalds

The Storm In Me

What is the dark news father,
That you know so well,
Cold and clear:
A wind shivers the bones.

DARK PINES - -

Softness, ashes.
The trees brittle with ice
Under moonlight,
The full dark tides move me.

What is the wind father,
A wind that turns the bones to ashes,
The bones of my skull to jewels,
Your eyes, glazed, meet mine.

Father, the storm in me, that wild
Blood dark and corrosive in my veins.
Father, diamonds of my rage
Cut your creases in my face.

Miriam Kessler

Beyond Belief

Nothing stays in my mind.
I ask you twice, and
twice again. What did you say?
and you say it again,
though less patiently than

before. I remember only I've forgotten.
Things run
together, uncontrolled,
like a watercolor
painted by an amateur.

Dank weather settles in my brain
as on that day when,
six years old, I looked up
at the twelfth floor
hospital window, where

a bandaged head
looked down. My father said

it was my mother,
and you're supposed
to believe your father. But

that day I bought
doubt
by the barrelful,
and never believed again
till one

year later, when
I read her name on stone.

Merrill Leffler

Farewell

In these faces it is always farewell.
You may see yourself here or not.
You may walk a straight line to hell
And arrive through the front door or knock

Without thinking at the back.
You may be schooled in caution like a spy
And count every step and still backtrack
Into the arms of the enemy.

You may crawl on your knees for a hundred years
And engrave a yellow star on your breast.
You may try and cover your fears
And pretend that you have come to a rest.

Dear friends, we are traveling this way
Alone. Finally, there are no lies.
Minute by minute, day by day,
Each life is a blessing, each blessing a disguise.

DARK PINES - - -

Janice Lynch Schuster

Run, Baltimore-Washington International Airport

September 11, 2001

When the man yells, "Run!"
exits disappear
people fall
to the ground
you move along
middle-aged and plump,
terrified, and this life,
which had exhausted you for days,
is abruptly too precious to lose.

You run and wait
for the red tile walls to collapse
trapping you at the door,
(you should have exercised more).

This life flashes
before your eyes—
you've heard it would.
Only it is no montage,
no highlights at eleven,
just the clear and present moment
of all you love:
children and husband
faces crowded on memory's screen
real-time and real:

You run for this life
because you have no other.

Ann B. Knox

I Dream Old Dylan Came Back

He scratched at the kitchen door,
clicked across the tiles with his low-
slung swag. I squatted to circle his neck,
feel his body curve in welcome—same
red collar, same lop-ear shriveled
from a fight. Remember, we bathed it,
hands touching over the open wound.

Where have you been? It's ten years since
we buried you in the meadow, there's
a hollow where the mower leaves grass
ragged and berries invade the stubble.

Must I rearrange my life now, set out
your waterbowl, your scrap of carpet?
Do you come back to remind me I've been
too long without this rise of gladness,
that welcome lay too long unused?

But you'll leave again. Besides, I have
grown accustomed to my own order—books,
the hard blue hills. I'm glad you came,
I miss you, but don't stay, don't stay.

Elizabeth Sullam

At Grandmother's Fountain

Caravans of thought pass
still pass still through the ring
of the mind, limpid as the water
that flows out of the mask's
deceiving mouth, wavers
as it falls and dissolves

DARK PINES --

fleetingly in the last shell
of the fountain.
Our times pass too
leaving no trace in this oasis
that borders another kingdom,
where a circle of water contains
all our fantasies in its hollow.
And past hours ambiguous
and worn, grow old
in a nymph's cold breast.

Lillian Frankel

Dance Class

I am waiting for my turn
to leap across the floor
as Lucille Fisher, the teacher,
plays the piano.

She nods to me.
"Now it's your turn
to do your leaps."

I jump out from the group
of child dancers
and leap.
I hang onto the air

just as my mother did
the week before
when she ran out into the street
after a burning child.

Just as my uncle did
when he gathered all the holy books,
then ran to the dried up well
to hide them from the Nazis.

I leap across the room,
almost kicking the walls,
never stopping.
Lucille Fisher wildly pounding the piano
to keep me in the air.

The dancers cheer,
clap their hands.

And my mother is running and leaping,
pulling off her coat
to smother the flames.

We stand over Rosie
as she lies
wrapped in the old red coat.

They take her away,
leaving the charred coat
impaled on the wooden fence.

We walk home slowly.
Then my mother says,
"If only I could have run a little faster."

And I dance and I leap
faster and faster.
I know I will never stop.

Tamara Gawthrop

Translating a Decline and Fall

Whether: Disease returning to
"active duty," or the force of age,
this overthrow comes in your blood.
The conqueror's language is bitter
with consonants of medical terms
for: "There's only so much we can do."

DARK PINES -

The stuttering tongue of defeat
won't be the last voice you hear calling
(stranger in your own body)
I shall stay and translate for you.

When written words quit making their sense
I'll let poetry stand in my eyes.
When your sight goes—listen for me
whispering sunsets in your ear.
I'll bring the music of an aspen's touch
when no more voices can reach you,
and then save what you cannot hold onto.
I won't turn away until you're gone—
but translate the silences to myself.
This love shares no language with good-bye.

Joseph Thackery

In the Barn

I remember dark and the stink of the sick hog.
Watch a beast dying, he takes on a human face,
as if life could not let go. But as for the rest,
I don't remember whether we burnt him or gave him
to his kind, who'll eat anything. I only know
that knowing love only from Uncle Billy's Smokehouse
Monthly, I clutched him with what passed for lover
knees, turned his shrieking grin toward medicine
in a whiskey bottle and thought of how some day I'd...

He didn't choke, just went woman-limp; then came
a wooden stillness, a bluing of the eyes as I let him
easy down. What I remember best is the pigeons,
cooing unseen, unconcerned in the shadowing rafters.

Anne Sheldon

Will You Miss Me When I'm Gone?

(a line from an Appalachian folksong)

Why anyone would marry,
subject the self
to another self within four walls
remains a mystery.
See them bruised and bruising?
And in the wake
of these collisions
bits adhere. A part of one
becomes a part
of another's cheek.
Ribs so lightly lodged
between opposing ribs
begin to fuse. Thus,
when one leaves or dies,
another's skin is ripped away.
Blood is freed. This absence is pain
and can't be overlooked.

If, on the other hand,
human contact only happens
outside the wreath of dried things
on your door, rest assured
the household objects will mourn you
for a certain time.
The wine glass will remember,
till it's washed,
the imprint of your lips.
Till someone comes to strip the bed,
the dented pillow will recall
your last bewildered dream.
The pages of this
half-read book will taste
your finger-sweat for years.

Roland Flint

Skin

If the wood is good grain,
And the carpenter, the fit, the caulking,
The cask will be good
And if the grapes are good
The wood and the wine
Will improve each other,
In the dark long days of aging.

The separate tastes of earth
Will taste again and change again each other,
Until, like membrane, somehow
In and between the wood and wine
There will be no separation,
Wood from dark from wine.

When this goes on, anything can happen.
Go back, go back to mystery.
Now I am grateful to my small poem
For teaching me this again:
That my God is still the moment
Where the wood is no longer itself,
Where the wine is no longer, only, itself.

Anne Becker

Ode

We are all words
broken like *teeth*
riddled with *holes*.

What are *apple* words?
black words, *red* words?
words of *ivory*, of *clay*

golden words like *orange's*
radiant table
as *fleshy* as *earlobes*

supple as *skin*
travel as
wave. particle.

Waitress of Light
we pay our own
ransom. rejoice.

Valerie Jean

Thread

Between two women who love
the moon, looking into the night
from separate cities, the sky hangs
pregnant with prayer. Their lives
and stories drift off the pages

of their letters the way wet kisses
of loud lovers drip off the edges
of pillows into their dreams.
Words sift through the dark times
and punctuate those screaming

white days, when the world cracks
and shifts on ground as fluid as
the sea, but the women gazing up
at the stars see brilliance in each
other's hearts and can imagine

themselves whole. Those old still
rumbling fears beaten into their skins
dissipate into the sweet lyrics of
laughter. Purple crocuses set out
on the kitchen counter of the one

become background landscaping
for yellow lilies bordering the fence
of the other. These women sew
a sacred quilt between them, using
light bouncing off the moon as thread.

Patric Pepper

Fantastic Creature

Crawling from under the sod so that it might breathe,
  slinking across wet pavement this drizzly day,
pulpy and helpless, no bravery before our shoes,
  automobiles, and the blade-beaked robins of spring,
heading for somewhere, wherever not quickly enough,
  pulling its length and its weight, such burden of being,
stopping and lifting a blind end up to this world,
  home in the raw March day of this infinite life,
heedless of us, and our tires, and the harrowing birds,
  wordlessly yanking its only effects to no destiny,
being-but-being, O role model, mentor and muse

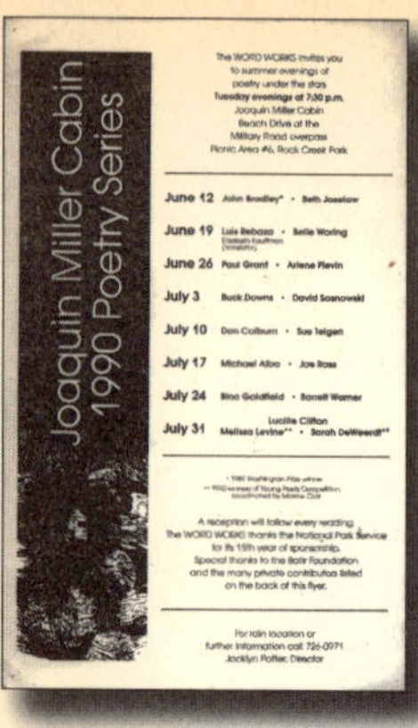
Joaquin Miller Cabin
1990 Poetry Series

The WORD WORKS invites you
to summer evenings of
poetry under the stars
Tuesday evenings at 7:30 p.m.
Joaquin Miller Cabin
Beach Drive at the
Military Road overpass
Picnic Area #6, Rock Creek Park

June 12 John Bradley* • Beth Joselow
June 19 Luis Rebaza • Belle Waring
June 26 Paul Grant • Arlene Plevin
July 3 Buck Downs • David Sosnowski
July 10 Don Colburn • Sue Teigen
July 17 Michael Albo • Joe Ross
July 24 Bina Goldfield • Barrett Warner
July 31 Lucille Clifton, Melissa Levine** • Sarah DeWeerdt**

* 1989 Washington Prize winner
** 1990 winners of Young Poets Competition, coordinated by Maxine Clair

A reception will follow every reading.
The WORD WORKS thanks the National Park Service
for its 15th year of sponsorship.
Special thanks to the Bair Foundation
and the many private contributors listed
on the back of this flyer.

For rain location or
further information call 726-0971
Jacklyn Potter, Director

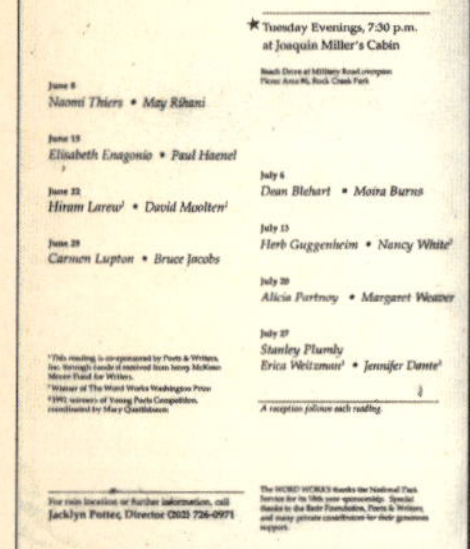
Joaquin Miller Cabin
Poetry Series 1993

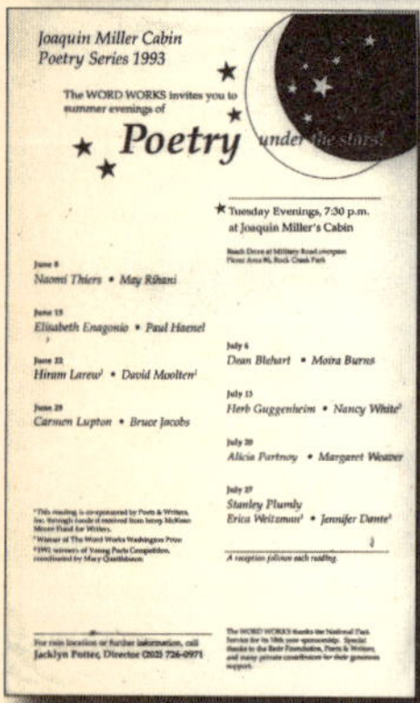

The WORD WORKS invites you to
summer evenings of

Poetry under the stars!

Tuesday Evenings, 7:30 p.m.
at Joaquin Miller's Cabin

June 8
Naomi Thiers • May Rihani

June 15
Elisabeth Enagonio • Paul Haenel

June 22
Hiram Larew[1] • David Moolten[1]

June 29
Carmen Lupton • Bruce Jacobs

July 6
Dean Blehart • Moira Burns

July 13
Herb Guggenheim • Nancy White[1]

July 20
Alicia Partnoy • Margaret Weaver

July 27
Stanley Plumly
Erica Weitzman[2] • Jennifer Dante[2]

A reception follows each reading.

For rain location or further information, call
Jacklyn Potter, Director (202) 726-0971

ABOVE: Poets Moshe Dor and Barbara Goldberg share books with Jack Magarrell and others, at a reading in 1992.

RIGHT: Carmen Lupton and Bruce Jacobs, 1992.

BELOW: Beth Joselow and 1989 Washington Prize winner John Bradley at 1990 series opening.

RED STARS---

II

"LET THE RED STARS FALL!"

—Joaquin Miller

OP: Buck Downs reading in 1990.

BOVE: Lucille Clifton delights an udience of 140 in honor of the 1990 oung Poet winners.

ELOW: Grace Cavalieri at Miller's Cabin.

POETS READING 1990-1995

Above, from the top: Don Colburn read his prize-winning poem about the act of presenting his poetry for critical respons at a workshop, July 1990.

Center: Poetry lovers gather at a reception.

Bottom: Lyubomir Nikolov checks the mike with Jacklyn at his reading in 1995

RED STARS---

Stanley Plumly

Altitude

—Ten-, twelve-, twenty-story clouds stacked
just south of here. My mother's mother's father
in too-bright ocean sunlight trying to teach
angle and foil, lift and flow, the sailshape
of a wing. —Not to imagine anything higher
yet connected, nor how the string tightens
yet goes slack at the rise and set, the wind
moving on a line like a wave. —Almost mortal,
still coming down the stairs learning to walk,
bicycle clips and cap, ready to ride
the bike bought from the Wrights in Dayton,
eighteen ninety-something, back in the ocean
mist that rises behind us. —Bicycle
wheels with wings, the bicycle brothers lucky.
And lucky to have a camera, in winter black
and white, one of them flying, the other timing.
—To stand on the coast of this part of Carolina
in summer is to join the wind. In December,
the leeward to landward, shipwreck side.
—For a man to fly he moves across and out
and never stops. Only Orville-in-the-air
holds on, nineteen forty-eight, the post-war,
Cold War year one of us survives. —The granite
Wright Memorial, visible from sea, the grave-
stone where they start, first with the gliders,
then with the power, and tracks along a line
to sail a train. —Someone taking pictures
of the two flying kites (boxy, triangular,
sailcloth blown to rags) that look like,
in the blur of the turn of the century, ours.

-1990-1995

Margaret Weaver

Gravity

Her arms are still "Swan Lake," her head "Giselle,"
her light steps trained in years of dance.
She remembers height, sky under her feet,
thinks of Chagall's painted villager soaring
with cows and roosters over moonlit roofs.

She has seen moons rising in Japan,
flights of geese arrowing the sky,
monarchs air-borne to the world's end,
their spotted orange wings dyeing the hills.
She cuts out photographs

of ordinary people leaving earth:
divers leaping up before they plunge,
an outfielder launched after a homer
roaring over the fence, skaters
spinning above partners.

Past eighty now, still moved by music,
she walks with care, does not forget
the call, the lift of rising notes,
the dazzle of steps learned and taught
to those who now come forward offering flowers.

She remembers flying, wingless, poised
in that instant when anything is possible
before the solidity of landing
and the need to move first one foot,
then the other, always forward.

RED STARS-

Marie Pavlicek-Wehrli

Song for the Trains and the Small, Lost Towns

I'm singing to the trains in my head tonight,
they light out beyond the rim of Matta's hill,
follow the Monongahela along its blighted
shores, the tunnels and watchtowers, stacks of the steel
mills shine like hard metal buttons behind my eyes.
I'll write a symphony of hissing tracks and clanging
water, by the rivers in my skull no town ever dies,
each crossing is clear and every thing bears the mark of a hand.
Who would I tell where I go as I lie here alone?
The window opens out over a flowering hedge, it's spring;
along the rails, winter's dried brush cracks and drifts, stones
spray as the engines speed left and right, who'd know why I sing
of twisting curves and matchbox towns? It's all gone
now but for here, in this room, where I sing.

David Moolten

Housatonic

This particular memory defies
The history that followed it simply
By carrying on in its own good time
Where dry road clay still blows
Through the headlamps of my father's bounding Jeep
On the way to night-fish in the Housatonic.
I believe a boy might just imagine
If he's young and naive enough
That all that bright dust has blown
Up into the mist of stars
He sees later on the jetty creaking
The drowned woodwinds of its pilings,
The way he might believe a prayer
Frail as a feather lure in his fluty voice
Which begins "Our Father who art in heaven,"

Refers to a man who smokes Winstons
And Vaselines his hair. It's been so long
I can't say for sure. I will say
That I loved the ignition of things,
Chasing lightning bugs with an old relish jar
Down by the water while my father
Kissed his hands into moments of brilliance
Putting a match to each chain smoked cigarette.
Well, the fireflies died black and dry
As cloves, and I struck out across the years
Of his women, his moods, and his general intolerance,
And what escapes a fire anyway
Is just smoke, a flight of ashes,
And what are ashes anyway but the dust
Everything spoken or written says we are
Like my father dying with each bad habit
Into a man. But just now he stands
Bright as his hands above that black river
When I think of him, so that's what I believe
As if caught in the right light
Some dust can burn forever.

Arlene Plevin

Memory

There are yellow voices in the kitchen.
Outside the window, all the team captains
who ever picked me last
press noses to the warm glass.
In the distance, a chorus of relatives.

On beige packing boxes they perch,
hopeful as steps.
My uncle swivels and bows—tuxedo tails float
like an apostrophe.
His reckless hands sweep the crowd.
A breath, at once they sing—

RED STARS-

recipes for love, for money,
for meatloaf.

The family's oldest sycamore shades them
and the garden.
Fat tomatoes, fatter worms, and grasshoppers,
green as heart-shaped peppers.

Ah, lush garden,
sweet gangster.
There are daffodils here, my favorite.
A marsh smell, a golden throat, and wings.

David Moolten

Having Come This Way

What is memory if not a sense of direction?
Those geese on Cochituate's blue paper lake
Perfectly still as it began to flare
With sun laid directly against it
As if there were a fiery furnace
In which all living things live
With the perfect faith needed
And every moment of the past tested and retested
In that kind of crucible, and the geese
With their sudden fluttering sense of home
Not trying to evade it, but feeling their way
Towards its available fire,
Clumsily, noisily, like all our wishes and hopes
Wondering if they should take this breeze
And where, riding the laziness of the day
Up into great sheets of lucid air
Then skimming the flaming water once more.
But the lightest hours travel farthest
And only when I look back now
Through the arches of rooms with no ceilings
That become the softly ruddying trees

Do the geese drift farther and farther
In their own warm light,
As if deciding at last
As if always flying south when I think of them.

Hiram Larew

If He Never Hears This

There's no pattern to what disappears
Nothing to make sure that our ideas are everlasting
Or repeated
The puny overlap between us all is such that
We can't predict what stays or lingers
Or leaves
It may be that wishing wells
Especially their walls
Know all about our yearning to endure
Somehow fireworks do too coming down
But mostly we know that everyone we know
Is just water
And all we are is snaps

Never ask anyone anything directly
Be a swan's neck
So that you find out everything by guessing
And for balance
Imagine loving someone so much that it feels like
You are unscrewing the lid of a jar
Before going

The boring point is this
The best friend to make is chance
Do whatever it takes
To wake up tangled in the arms of maybe
Start to trust what you've done
For as long as a blink
Mostly think like a windy corner.

Kenneth Carroll

Riding Shotgun

You riding shotgun, grandma said
my face glazed over with ignorance
in all my 12 years I had never heard such a thing
riding shotgun? I repeated seeking an explanation
all I knew was that I was sitting next to grandpa in the front seat
close enough to smell his hi-karate after-shave &
trace the veins in his hands as they knitted like winding creeks
around his slender fists & unfurled as long rivers up his arms
the front seat with grandpa, a rare allowance for a child born
in a time when a lack of reverence for any adult
could find your behind burning from an adroit switching

in the backseat my jealous brothers & sisters rolled their eyes
snaking their tongues furiously out of their mouths to mock me

grandma broke the term down-riding shotgun
there was something john wayne-ish about it
something my cowboy & indian playing ass could dig
the image was phat,
I imagined myself, Nat Love of the projects
afro peeking out from the brim of my Stetson
steel faced, eagle eyed brother, winchester
between my legs, scouring the horizon for
bandits & navajo

I wish I could have seen the cancer coming that took grandma
or the alcoholism that would steal my father's eyes from me
but my job was simple, to make sure the coast was free
of obstruction for grandpa's bifocal maneuverings as
we headed to our ancestral grounds in upper marlboro

what ya see boy, asked grandpa intermittently
even when it was obvious he needed no help
my eyes spinning like the pontiac's hubcaps, never leaving
the road
I answered simply
it's all clear over here grandpa
& it was as far as I could see.

Don Colburn

Wildflowers

Until I heard the names in my own voice
I never saw them whole: chickweed, toothwort,
May apple, Dutchman's breeches, Indian pipe.
A list was my father's way of witnessing;
it made a flower real. And this afternoon
in the weedy meadow by the towpath,
I'm jotting odd names on a scrap of paper
for no one in particular, myself maybe
or my father. Back then I let him teach me
to look down at the ground for stars,
bells, shades of blue. He was never happier
than when we looked up accuracy's myriad names
and he wrote them out in slanted letters.
Now, over and over, like a child,
I say *gill-over-the-ground, gill-*
over-the-ground, gill-over-the-ground,
and in the saying see it blossom again
inside its spilled blue name.

Paul Haenel

I Think of Your Birthday while Cutting Tenons

I was sleeping earlier today with the TV on
and there was a tornado a wind so ferocious
people were yelling and shingles were spinning

in the air and I dreamed for the first time
in a long time of my father   who told
a story all his life about the one tornado

he saw   how they were coming back
from golfing and the sky blackened
and got still and then there it was

I was a baby but grew up scared
of vacuums as if it had happened to me
grew up fearing the moment the black

sky would turn green and leaves
turn over like animals showing
their bellies in supplication

Tonight I was cutting tenons
and you appeared in a boat out of nowhere
a wave and a smile in the dead calm

I had to look down at my hands
and the wide blade chewing up
what I slowly pushed into it

and I thought of vacuums and Kansas
and looked away the blade kept spinning
In Kansas perhaps a jay would just

have landed on the grass which you
washing dishes and humming could see
out your window while maybe west of you

a high dark anvil of cloud would be gathering strength
and you wouldn't know wouldn't think
of the boat out there coming for you

May Rihani

Palm Trees

Do you think Palm Trees dream?
What resides in their minds?
Do you think the Palms of Texas yearn for the Palms of Baghdad?
Which ones departed? Which migrated?
Are they twins, carrying between them a long mirror
Reflecting the character of the West, reflecting the face of the East;
Searching for a magical thread that links the far corners with each other?

-1990-1995

Do you think the Palm chants in solemn silence
Words about the similarities in the mirror?
Do you think they whisper to the Earth in solemn Silence
Do not lose Hope?

Perhaps this is what makes the Earth a bead in the rosary of a dervish
  that is eternally turning.
Spinning invisible threads that link the caravans of humanity.

Translated from the Arabic by Zuheir Al Faqih

Lyubomir Nikolov

Fire

No matter how you lay it on the fire
wood is beautiful
when it burns.

Alone, it is still beautiful.

But I like the brotherhood of twigs, logs, leaves.

I like the fire to remind me of the tree
before the ax stripped it.

And as in some strange camera obscura
where nature is reversed,
I see the tree replenish itself in the flames.

Down below, in the ashes, shine leaves.
Up from them grow the branches,
then the trunk,
and roots glide out through the chimney
to stroll among the onrushing clouds.

Translated from the Bulgarian by Jane Cooper

Barri Armitage

Fall Ritual

Even the marigolds on my window sill
speed on to seed, showing it's time
to shorten the path to earth.
You always stay at twenty-two,
you, the expert at shortcuts:
three cakes in one bowl,

four quilt squares, or eight, at a time.
Your bike, faster than cars at rush hour,
seemed almost welded to you,
sped you along the night's straight edge,
armlight blinking gold,
until a Chevy cut you short.

Outside, I soften a groove in the clay.
Maroon and gold petals, dry as confetti,
slip away at the slightest touch.
I wriggle the seeds apart
and push them into a common bed.
Reluctant to cover up,

I savor the feel of earth,
then sprinkle it, pack it like snow.
Bone of my bone, you were packed in me,
grew from meat I chewed, from milk I drank—
seed buried in seed
you carried to the ground.

When snow's patches have melted
and the flurry of birds returns
like the rush of rain,
I will kneel at this earth's pocket
as flesh of the springtime's flesh
begins to crown.

Martin Galvin

The Big Leagues

Since, being left handed, he couldn't play
second base, he caught a leaf, a single Vee-
veined leaf, and then, from a bird
who had flied out

he caught a white feather, and once
a fish that flopped in his hand
and lay still as a spent penny,
one eye at a time accusing him,
him who played left field, flat-eyed
as a window at what is coming.

He caught an acorn from a prudent squirrel
and tucked it in his pocket to keep the cold
coins company, caught a hint the season
was over.

He caught a faint drumbeat, a sign
the rain is kind enough to let him hear
when there is nothing on the dugout roof
but itself and the late September night,
those soft reminders,
those polished catchers.

Gail Collins-Ranadive

Pacific

As if she could
take all back into
herself, the ocean
rolls over the land as fog.
The Bay's gone,
and buildings. Trees

become kelp
to the otters. We're

not alone this
time in the womb: the rhythmic
beating in our ears is
the barking of sea lions.
In the dense, deep cold, whales
hold their breaths
for as long as they
can. When they surface

we're there, aware
that their grace-filled return
to the seas is without us.

Patricia Bertheaud

The River

A woman with a child strapped to her back
holds a pole in her hand
to measure the depths
and the shallows, the mud and water
covering a short pole, a deep walker.
Water past the hem of her skirt
up to her knees.
She is slipping down
and rising from all fours
from the cement bank of the river
that goes numb with sunlight
and the shadows of bent knees.
I'd like to crack the sun
make the river go blind and dry
for its own sake.
The river didn't ask for this;
the red-orange dye
that floats from her skirt,
or the man on the other side

1990-1995

who wades in his own urine.
The river didn't ask to speak
with such a thick tongue.
The jingle of loose change
that falls from her skirt
into water is silenced.
The child on her back looks down.
The river has nothing to do with drowning.

Naomi Thiers

Never With the Mouth

"I was bred for slaughter
like the other animals
to suffer exactly at the center
where there are no clues except pleasure"
—Linda Gregg

The ferns and shags, the ancientness playing
among us, don't talk of it, talk of it all night, never
with the mouth, awareness resting in the belly,
the rounded belly the marketplace hates.
Give me the rigor there, the ripped field,
the evil abundance of twins or the angel
of barrenness. Red leaves singing for release.
Release will not come. Swallow the aching
whole. Draw breath. Never with the mouth.
Burn my mouth. Burn my words
in split water, love, in the night tremendous
split my tongue in black weeds.

Gary Moody

Inskaya

Through starlight and coal ash raining from the unscrubbed stacks of Inskaya, I track what can only be elk. They have been running through autumn's first snow. Skinless birch saplings have been crushed under their flight. A spike of larch holds fur, still heavy, unfrozen and wet from the run. I must be near.

Only after I stumble upon them in a sheltering windfall of red Siberian pine can I tell they are only two, a cow and bull. Is she his mate, or he her calf? Are they lost? Have they wandered from the sheltering Taiga, or have they somehow existed, hidden, yet so close, sensed only as shadows in starlight? All their life

long has been running. Shelter to shelter. Until now. What holds them now and their animal heart's steadfast refusal to run, either before the other? Have we ever been so close to that which we most fear until now, each breath we take finally tangible in the cold? And the forbidden scent of the stranger, a heat almost visible in the lens which separates

the three of us in this cusp of dark. The animal eye, the iris in starlight, breath and pollen of burning coal.

Minnie Bruce Pratt

The Blue Cup

Through binoculars the spiral nebula was
a smudged white thumbprint on the night sky.
Stories said it was a mark left by the hand
of Night, that old she, easily weaving
the universe out of milky strings of chaos.

Beatrice found creation more difficult.
Tonight what she had was greasy water

whirling in the bottom of her sink, revolution,
and one clean cup.

She set the blue cup
down on the table, spooned instant coffee, poured
boiling water, a thread of sweetened milk. Before
she went back to work, she drank the galaxy that spun
small and cautious between her chapped cupped hands.

David Kresh

Goodnight. Goodnight.

Outside your hotel room window, look,
I am wrapping the steel stars in velvet.
Close your sharp eyes.

Tumbled and spun
like sheets washed and dried,
now fold in on yourself,
clean and hot.
What was stiff,
red with dried blood,
is softer, an unsigned
brown painting.

I am sending you
a black envelope. The handsome
blank stamp is one in
The Forgotten American Artists Series.
(You could never fit them all
into your album with its empty
hinges rustling
like desiccated bees' wings.)

In the envelope is the green moon's
return ticket.

Fred Marchant

Night Heron Maybe

We woke to more rain, sheets of it,
and I felt in the dark for how wet
the sill had become. Then I rolled back
to the radio, its evangelical preacher
and his whisper of inevitable sin.
Lightning surprised the innocent shore,
and the thunder was a hollow sound,
like that a bone will make breaking.

I do not know the names of birds by song,
and I do not know if this is the one
that sang, but out of the estuary
and the darkness, came a long, sleek,
and pointed call, as if one bird knew
what the given world gave, and wanted more.

James Hopkins

the devil beating his wife

the storm came down the river
like a bad husband,
banging from mountain to mountainside,
bloated and mumbling something black.
low-slung clouds,
hanging like fists in the heat.

and summer, on her back
on a red plastic raft,
floating with her toes in the drink.
the sun beating down.
a green dragonfly.
and pretty much nowhere to hide.

god i hate it
when he's like this, she thinks.
her arm glistens in the light.
she wonders about closing her eyes,
and slipping under.
ponders leaving for good
in the fall.

thunder. and lightning.
he's squalling in the treetops
cracking the air like a whip.
heat and darkness mixing to silver.
and summer
toweling off on the bank

remembers the bedroom windows—
all wide open.
now there'll be hell to pay.
she's hoping it won't take long this time.
the first droplets hitting
her face.

Mark Wallace

Like the Sky is Poking Holes in my Arms

We set the mattress outside,
lit candles on its corners
and waited for rain.
The water fell, abundant, not like that
which sits around me now,
and it was hard to recall
the labors of silence.
The chance that is the sky
said this would bring no end to watching.
Have you too lay down
where the smallest sound hovers
on the edge of pistols and reports

like the sudden flap of a wing
to know yourself as strong as the skin?
It is close to what, together,
we had no chance for, even to lose.
I have been strung, furious
for illusion, while silence in the inner ear
suggests what never will happen.
In the dream we set tables
and welcomed doors and guests,
listening hard through news of storms
for a story we could take to ourselves.
It only happened that way once
or each time we didn't expect,
the magic open, the ritual
of flesh. We set the mattress outside
and leaned among, and waited, and leaned.

Carmen Lupton

Afterflood

I slogged through lakes to get
beyond the highways.
Each curve turned into a situation
dying for attention and lace.
No, I can't drink.
My words were chunks of liver,
blasted by heavenly structure
but now my voice is butter.
Without soreness,
I sing to hold god in my mouth.
Even while hearts are nailed to the fence
I hear the cadence of each beat.
Love explodes & is tender as an infant's shoe,
begs us to walk down the street,
slip in and out of caves
listen to the dead in the heavy rain
absorb the stain of water.

--1990-1995

Luis Rebaza-Soraluz

The Keys

The one who obtains the keys
will not gain the door
He is master of a formula
Of a breath

And the one whose hands
are forged by steel
knows not in truth
their weight

Toss them as he may
into the garden of night
And testimony exists
Or a body lies there

Another sex is a key
An eye of the needle
A reddish spiral
The rapping upon another breast

The one who gains the keys
has not trodden the doorsill
He is lord without lands
He is a wing of the covenant

And the one who clutches the bunch
to his breast-plate
Has not defended the passage
Has not penetrated the orchard

The epic is a kingdom
at the door
that the hands
may not touch

And he paces the garden
with charred hands

forever transient through
the door he doesn't own

Ah let's take the step
that unveils
what has been taken away
The side that is hidden

Carried through by the keys

By their anchor in the body

David Biespiel

Mount Tabor

These lines, like slanted rain, on the East side of the river, below the dormant mountain: Here, in a place
I never knew as a child, the old women sit with their knitting and pluck yarn as if stripping
Feathers off a chicken. Or, other days, dog-earring their Corinthians, their Job and Solomon's Songs.
These lines sing or slaughter. These lines dream of decaying birds and the silent speech that flies, like a summer, all over the world.

Neither day nor night plunders a mountain. Neither day nor night reverses the aging gardens
Forgotten in the footnotes of expert treatises on time. Even lovers who walk along the emptied volcano
Know this is how it started: words and love, like roses, for hands or tombs. It'll never end,
And so now the children come and, without pain, picnic in the grass, the old women watch them as if in a changeless dream

That, even late in life, having passed through many doors, imprisons them, with a new faith, afresh.

John Bradley

Where I Live

In memory of William Stafford

I live on the corner
of Ninth and Lewis, the last
house on the last corner
of the last block. I live

in that house where moss
and morning glories conspire
to topple the porch. I live

in that slab of light
you see suspended
in the night. Once inside
I'm no different

than any other
visitor to any other
star. That's what I love

about this story.

Craig McEldowney

sub-utopia (parodies of walden)

we carve our lines across her pregnant, rounded belly
  anxiously swiping up our pieces of cake
    to sequester
      behind split shank fences
        and chain-link repentance
            throwing up trees like wet cotton candy
              to swab away the clouds
                —alcohol before the hypodermic—
                  and to write clearly in invisible ink
                                    'this land is my land'

RED STARS

we sweep by
our stealth puppies dropping land mines
on recon strolls
through enemy sidewalks
as we mow the sprawling lawns
of our caged islands
with long black driveways.

Joanne "Rocky" Delaplaine

Assume the Can Opener

Assume the can opener
is how the economist in the joke
proposed to save himself, a priest, and a lawyer
after prayer and logic failed
to open the canned food
that washed to the shores of their deserted island.

Assume that people are good and worth saving
said my economist father
who flew away to a foreign land and died
trying to feed a starving world
with a pencil and a slide rule.

I grew thin assuming he would return
to this deserted island,
can opener in hand,
to feed me

until the dog-hungry day I
followed my nose, grabbed two rocks
and knew:

I had all I'd need
to open the cans and feast
with leftovers to spare
for any who hungered along.

Lucille Clifton

homage to my hips

these hips are big hips.
they need space to
move around in.
they don't fit into little
petty places. these hips
are free hips.
they don't like to be held back.
these hips have never been enslaved,
they go where they want to go
they do what they want to do.
these hips are mighty hips.
these hips are magic hips.
i have known them to put a spell on a man
and spin him like a top!

Mary Hilton

From "Freedom My Keeper"

With such force as to be startled. With such power as to be diverted. We fail to listen and in that an eternal regret. The instant mindfulness of our surroundings. How many times must I so angered by the repetition when the break a routine that is signaling must I refuse that one thing out of the ordinary must I too fail experience alone for one year more? Yes and thankful. Had I only been more aware we could have avoided such heightened blasphemies.

And I will make the mistake again. And I will make the mistake again again. Not in this which it is correct but then I will refuse to learn through knowing. Again. Again. Anything.

RED STARS--

Grace Cavalieri

The Door That Opens Inward

Disappointment is fur that sticks
in your throat, starts small,
then becomes a smooth
shiny ball.
We study its velocity by running
from it.
We go to other countries to learn a
new language.
We laugh about it, pretending
to understand how it works—We
form clubs and societies, ideas become
television and radio, turning
blue, red, and green—but at the center
of the hard surface, no color
but the one we tried to throw away.
The manufacturer makes
better and better samples. It is there
drenched with sadness—belonging
to someone else—
someone always hugely successful with it.
The star is on the other
side of the door, oh
if we could take it,
receive the afterlight into ourselves,
here, with loving care of all we are not writing
for fear of disappointment.

Beth Baruch Joselow

Sexy Shoes

Ingathering at the corner
of siren and dread,
last to join the long list.

Dancing the hot step.
Stripes. More food than
anyone can possibly in
so little time,   more
space than anyone can
                    rattle around in
less.

The wheat rains
hard and fast, faster,
fast, light as snow.

Spiritual traffic
at ground level
flagging, fasting,
facing
prevailing winds,
transfusions, bulletins
and transfers, air
and light.

Nancy Johnson

Side Show

On tiny patent leather shoes the fat lady balances.
Her toes kiss the dirt as she sits spread
voluminous-legged on a cranky wood chair.
Don't you want to grab puffs of her flesh,
roll them in your hands for texture?

A woman like this doesn't disappear
and if she did, those hot kisses would last
forever imprinted on the side show dust.
Kisses forever—the dream of children
jettisoned, ballooned by their mothers,

sent off with nothing, to where life becomes
all levels of people visiting back and forth—

the queen from zone five to the lion-faced twins—
crossing time and places, where a shot
to the head with a spike heel means being noticed.

Come to the side show now. Become a hologram
under glass, jumping rope in perpetual
motion, as if swiping at flies
that circle your head. You are etched
with a hologram tattoo—Tiger Jimmy

shimmering one fine layer above your skin,
whispering *tell her to give it back to you.*
Or you ride a Harley to the deaf end of a drive-in
where all pictures and no words spell
the precision of your travels without

Mother, I love you. The fat lady opens
her arms wide, offers a nipple from which to suck
your geography. The result is her edges riffle,
you leave a child, and it is impossible to tell
where the body begins and where it ends.

Margaret Hanzimanolis

GENE POOL / 3

Call it what you like:

gene emporium, quick change bazaar,
aquatic mall; it's nothing

but a pond, a pool,
around which mill
unborn, uncured and unendurable:

shoulder to shoulder
for that first historic dive.

1990-1995

You've heard them all along
circling the ancient watering hole.

You've seen their frantic, milling tracks—
their spoor, you know
it well: *deep dissatisfaction.*

Keep watching and you'll see the critical
transaction—a row of Esther Williams dives,
a surfacing.

(The press is there, flashbulbs go off.)
And then: a nervous splash of flutter kicks;

those in the first wave
cock their arms and pull themselves
through watery frontiers,

propelled, with hope and trepidation, toward
their better, healed, and perfect selves.

Gary Lilley

High Point

When I'm stoned I can see air, thin lines where
parts fit together. In the dark, my sight
becomes acute, particularly in
the foot of god space surrounding my head.
It's the gift of my age, and the knowing
a lot of dead people. I moved my life
in boxes in a yellow Ryder truck,
my return to this small town where Coltrane
once lived, loved, and now, there are two crossed streets
that carry his name. Listening to the jazz
on the gospel station, the horn and all
the min-wage worry, black in a bible
town factory, hard now as it was then.
The last trailer park remains, white only.

Mark Craver

Self-Portrait as a Tractor

Since I put the decals on the hood
this thing corners better
and takes hills with me leaning
opposite the gravity like a moon

buggy climbing up a crater.
What I see today: the elms
lose their leaves first. Tomorrow,
the oaks will start to die,

the paper will be late.
Yesterday I cut my knuckle
pulling jammed leaves
out between the mower deck

and the front axle. My cheek
against the warm hood, I backhanded
down and scraped the blade
without knowing until blood

dripped on the rusted yellow leaves.
It didn't happen then; it was
the next day, or the day after,
when I picked up a book

and broke the scab and the sting
made me see myself bent over
the tractor, head on the flying demon decal,
a man pasted on the world in the trivial

ouch of maintaining the machine
that maintains the machine
that sleeps and lets him get up
to mow the lawn. It happened

right then, holding that book,
I saw what I couldn't see
while I was riding the tractor:
It was the tractor riding me.

Michael Collier

The Barber

Even in death he roams the yard in his boxer shorts,
plowing the push-mower through bermuda grass,
bullying it against the fence and tree trunks,
chipping its twisted blades on the patio's edge.

The chalky flint and orange spark of struck concrete
floats in the air, tastes like metal, smells,
like the slow burn of hair on his electric clippers.
And smelling it, I feel the hot shoe of the shaver

as he guided it in a high arc around my ears,
then set the sharp toothy edge against my sideburns
to trim them square, and how he used his huge stomach
to butt the chair and his flat hand palming my head

to keep me still, pressing my chin down as he cleaned
the ragged wisps of hair along my neck.
A fat inconsolable man whose skill and pleasure
was to clip and shear, to make raw and stubble

all that grew in this world, expose the scalp,
the place of roots and nerves and make vulnerable,
there in the double mirrors of his shop, the long
stem-muscles of our necks. And so we hung below

his license in its cheap black frame, above the violet
light of the scissors shed with its glass jars
of germicide and the long tapered combs soaking
in its blue iridescence. Gruff when he wasn't silent,

he was a neighbor to fear, yet we trusted him
beyond his anger, beyond his privacy. He was like a father
we could hate, a foil for our unspent vengeance,
though vengeance was always his. He sent us back

into the world burning and itching, alive with the horror
of closing eyes in the pinkish darkness
of his shop and having felt the horse-hair brush, talc-filled,
cloying, too sweet for boyhood, whisked across the face.

RED STARS

Silvana Straw

The Acupuncturist

The acupuncturist says,
you have mole on your back
take it off
Chinese believe you have mole on your back you carry your past
big burden too heavy can't go forward.

The acupuncturist says,
you have mole on your neck
take it off
Chinese believe mole on your neck is like somebody choking you.
I can tell the way your tongue goes sssssssssss
your spirit is low
build your house on a circle
forget about childhood
don't take medicine.

My mom had a mole on her neck,
the year she took it off, she left my father.
I build my house on a circle where no hand can reach me.
My past is ugly, bumpy,
sometimes when I sleep it lies blind, tender,
quiet like a mole in the dark, except for the choking sounds.

I cherish the side effects,
the dark-colored fingerprint of the one who chokes me,
my eleventh year compressed into a heavy island on my back
that's only a quarter of an inch in diameter and
dark, dark like the woods dad threatened to disappear into
and never come back,
dark like the gun she pointed at him while he ironed,
dark like the voice coming out of her throat telling him to swear
to never call her crazy again.

Erica Weitzman

The Painter of Icons

Vinegar, verdigris-skinned, such sour
virginity, little mother, our lady
of the bony nose. Above in corona,
the pots of paint that are everything, that are
meaning in themselves with a flick of the wrist.
Daub on the eyes, paste-white. What a brush
to touch the nipple of a saint: mere horsehair.
A little miracle, this birth of things, things, things,
this transfer from life to life. And the customers,
clean palms crossed with cash, later ringing up
a diadem of red-glassed candles, scent of kerosene
and the oh have mercy on us-es for we are unbeloved
of the world. No wires, no mirrors needed
to produce such squalling. Just these plaques
of grooved wood, warped under water for antiquing,
real quality, there in the shallow tins where
light moves over like drugged fire. Ersatz
is a growth industry, indeed. Peel off the paint, just
the metal backing: such a thin basis, such nothing,
one wonders how it's done. Aha. There goes another.
One, eyes limned in tempera, off the line.

Elizabeth Alexander

Peccant

Maryland State Correctional Facility for Women,
Baltimore County Branch, has undergone a facelift.
Cells are white and un-graffitied, room-like, surprisingly airy.
This is where I must spend the next year, eating slop from tin trays,
facing women much tougher than I am, finding out if I am brave.
Though I do not know what I took, I know I took something.

RED STARS-

On Exercise Day, walk the streets of the city you grew up in,
in my case, D.C., from pillar to post, Adams-Morgan to Anacostia,
Shaw to Southwest, Logan to Chevy Chase Circles,
recalling every misbegotten everything, lamenting, repenting.

How my parents keen and weep, scheme to spring me,
intercept me at corners with bus tokens, pass keys, files baked in cakes.
Komunyakaa the poet says, don't write what you know,
write what you are willing to discover, so I will
spend this year, these long days, meditating on what I am accused of
in the white rooms, city streets, communal showers, mess hall,
where all around me sin and not sin is scraped off tin trays
into oversized sinks, all that excess, scraped off and rinsed away.

Buck Downs

Hot as steel rivets in girders braced flesh
thinking of your hand's touch and dry thunder
outside snapping pages of stiff air crash.
Look at me tremble. You are a wonder.
Like oil drained on asphalt makes tire tracks
easy to follow, the path your breath
makes straight across my mouth traces back
catachu eyes, I'm not sneezing, that means
the color, I don't mean your sleeping your eyes
I mean. My habit, plain things said the hardest
way around, we know now to call this
Proteus Complex, way to make a million
bucks. Let me chase the traces you breathe
out: it can't be too hot for me to live.

Colette Thomas

Providing Nourishment

It is, after all, a matter of discrimination—
certain mushrooms from poisonous others. Artichokes
and pomegranates from equally odd but inedible things.

Who is seated at the right hand, who eats first
in the life raft, or last. Expect the occasional

vampire at the banquet. Piranhas in the lily pond.
There are those who will embezzle what you would gladly

give away. They will thrive without your crème brulée.
Pearls from oysters, wheat from chaff. Here is the soup

kitchen, here is your ladle. The faces will sustain you,
their blistered knowing, etched shapes of empty mouths.

After thunder, rain. After rain, ten thousand insects.
You are closer than you think. The table is set.
The feast will arrive in its own sweet time.

Ally Acker

White Noise At Midnight

They all want me to stop talking to you.
My mother with the face of a television
blaring answers to the game no one ever guesses—
Bill Holden and Deborah Kerr in Bombay making nookie
on the graves. The wind cawing senseless to the Blue Moon.

Even you are tired of my chatter—Smart girl
your ears stuffed with happiness,
lying with your incest victim a year now

RED STARS--

you haven't sent me word as you promised, my darling
of second chances.

In the light graves the sheets are so clean.
I gather them up and sheath their silk
for bandages. When the armies arrive, Deborah
and Bill and I all lie and spread
for them. The way you liked me: stupid and silent.

We want to please them. We want every
thing absorbed—the liquids taken in like a sponge.
No messes. No white horses running wild at midnight.
Nothing fecund left to the brown fields. The blue

herons lift—their wings wild with applause. The moon turns
creamy. Everyone gets excited. There is nothing to do.
I cannot stop talking to you.

Terese Svoboda

How to Simplify Fractions

Put the big one
over the small one
and what do you get?
Don't tell.
He was a big man
and the first time
the boy cried.

Sometimes the wounded
use their scars.
Pull up the small one's
sleeves now, see all
the lines,
fine white
at the wrist,
where the answer goes.

Heather Davis

Showing Scars

Stand at the jukebox, contraposto,
shoving warm coins into a slot.
Some man will wobble close,
stomach protruding smooth as an egg
from his untucked workshirt.
In a hazy room lined with breasts
and yeasty breath he will want
to tell you about his wife, his life,
the scar on his arm. Sit down
with a cough, thoughts scattered
like pool balls. His eyes will be
glazed and thick-lashed, beautiful
as a woodland animal's. Ten
years in the pen for assault
with a deadly weapon and
he would do it again. Where the bullet
entered his own flesh, where he
accidentally shot himself, will be
a hole, the mark of his misdirection.
Where his beer spills will spread
a dark stain. Touch a finger
to the hardened wound. His buddies
will turn toward your corner,
then sidle over from their stools
with nudges and laughter.
Lean in slowly, whisper oh, my God
while each in his turn shows off
a limb and what it's missing.

RED STARS---

Grace Cavalieri

The Liberation of Music

When someone brought
Anthony Braxton flowers
He didn't ask if
They were
Picked off a tree

Like this tear
On my eye
Becoming a circle
Which I flick off my cheek
Just like that
With my nail

Removing the last flaw
Which holds my life together.

Marie Pavlicek-Wehrli

In the Valley of Fire, My Parents Are Sleeping

My mother stretched into transparency
after years of being riddled with longing,
nights, through the halls of our house she traveled,
a child cradled in each arm, a child stretched across her back,
strapped to her waist, a child in her head,
and beneath her ribs, the nubby seeds of fingers reaching.
Night was a smoky gray river she swam through,
her boat song-driven, the weight of her prayers filling
the space in the toes of her long black shoes;
when she sank, her side of the bed collapsed
against a floor already slanting into streets knee-deep
in soot and the glint of false diamonds.
When she was ready, she rolled toward the place

where gravity pulled, her eyes closed tight, in her chest,
the stoked fires of coal and cherry wood finally erupting.

In their bedroom at the back end of the house,
my father slept always on the side
of the bed nearest the door to the hallway.
Sleep was the stone heaviness he climbed into
each night, the creases of his hands still greased,
after washing, the hall's dim yellow light
softening the contours of his face as he tucked
his head down under the blanket's worn binding.
His body was solid, an opaque skin covering
a mechanism whose gears hummed discordantly,
the tiny links and brushes that informed
his feeling lay submerged in a vat of motor oil
and benzine, the fires he built still spill
from the rooms of our house, at night,
far away, I can glance out my window and see them.

Jay Rogoff

How We Came to Stand on That Shore

How we came to stand on that shore
I don't know, but in the failing
light whose particles sank in the sea
like diamonds, my father threw
his arm around me and walked me down
the beach. "This place was gorgeous then,"
he said, waving his free arm at
the shuttered mansions and concession
stands. "I loved your mother, then."
Tar and glass cluttered the beach.
A steaming smokestack stuck
in the ocean like a lipsticked
cigarette in a coffee cup.

Why
we came to walk on that shore I

RED STARS--

don't know except
for him to say, as before, "You
are the best thing I have done."
He'd stopped and stood stopping me.
"I've never told you this." The light
had nearly gone. Waves crept in
like sharkfins, dark against dark.
"When your mother and I vacationed
here, I know that there is where
you got started." I followed
his finger up to the boarded-up
window in the now burned-out hotel.

Barri Armitage

Square Dance

Blue-checked cotton made
to match, we court
and fluff like cranes.
Hip to hip we swing,
your eyes the pivot
for which there is no call.
In time, a change so gradual
I barely hear the moving
to another key—the words
that skip us on to split
the ring, to separate
and take the outside track,
circle up four until I stand,
birdie in the cage, pulled
to the grand right and left
by hands that slip on past.
"Gentlemen, walk single—
ladies, back to back—
remember your man as he comes
around the bend."
Costumes and bodies blur

until your face brings a lift of song—
the feel of the bones of your back,
arms circling me home,
swinging me round and round—
layers of slip lifting from my legs,
the two of us slowing the pace,
swinging the pure spin seen
from space—blue earth
banded with drifts of white.

Bruce A. Jacobs

The Black Advertising Copywriter Dresses for the Theater

The playwright explains
how she would like him:
Oxford shirt, Wrangler denims,
cowboy boots with silver heels.

She unfurls the smooth shirt
like a curtain, praises its weave
against her skin, tells him
if she were a client,
she'd admire his presentation.

With the mirror to her back
she is not Japanese.
She calls the woman in glass
"the way I look,"
like a tulip facing itself in water,
a rumor of liquid pastel.

The black advertising copywriter
nods, having been addressed
as "Yo, boss" by store clerks,
and quizzed about malt liquor
by people for whom
he provides a black friend.

He fastens six pearl buttons,
runs a zipper along her spine,
just for the moment,
since he knows
in late morning, she will lean
across cream sheets, a woman

who is not Japanese,
wearing the white shirt
of a black advertising copywriter
off her tawny shoulders,

and he will pull percale about his hips
exactly like a kimono,
ask her if she likes the way he looks
enough to walk with him through mirrors.

Dean Blehert

Holding Hands

"Dean Loves Pam"
Wet Cement Loves Hands
or hands love wet cement. But time and sunlight
harden the cement and callus the fingers,
and they no longer love each other, at least not
in that clingy way, though there's a kind of love
in galloping breathless over the sidewalk ("Beat you
to the fire hydrant on the corner!") and leaving
no discernible mark, no more than, on each other,
callused hands clapping to our singing.

Love is most at home with the yielding, but resilient,
the breast that seems to give way, give its all
to the hand, but a moment later is itself, ivory,
impervious. We want to be able to rend each other, swallow
each other like raw oysters, chew, twist, crush and know

by each other's moans that we have done so,
then have each other emerge, smiling, flawless,
like children pointing fingers and yelling **BANG BANG!**
—YOU'RE DEAD! —contorting, crumpling to the earth
to lie deadly still, then springing up laughing.

The handprint I leave in concrete outlasts the hand,
the thousands of handprints invisible
on the bodies of lovers (even white slap marks
now hidden in hardened eyes). Put your hand here,
if you can, into the impression. Can you feel
what my hand felt?

Jeffrey Harrison

Our Other Sister

for Ellen

The cruelest thing I did to my younger sister
wasn't shooting a homemade blowdart into her knee,
where it dangled for a breathless second

before dropping off, but telling her we had
another, older sister who'd gone away.
What my motives were I can't recall: a whim,

or was it some need of mine to toy with loss,
to probe the ache of imaginary wounds?
But that first sentence was like a strand of DNA

that replicated itself in coiling lies
when my sister began asking her desperate questions.
I called our older sister Isabel

and gave her hazel eyes and long blonde hair.
I had her run away to California
where she took drugs and made hippie jewelry.

Before I knew it, she'd moved to Santa Fe
and opened a shop. She sent a postcard
every year or so, but she'd stopped calling.

I can still see my younger sister staring at me,
her eyes widening with desolation
then filling with tears. I can still remember

how thrilled and horrified I was
that something I'd just made up
had that kind of power, and I can still feel

the blowdart of remorse stabbing me in the heart
as I rushed to tell her none of it was true.
But it was too late. Our other sister

had already taken shape, and we could not
call her back from her life far away
or tell her how badly we missed her.

Mary Quattlebaum

Cherry Tomatoes: Canning with My Sister

That summer blossomed with a bumper crop
of ruddy fruit the size of infant fists;
and while the oscillating fan blades chop-
chop-chopped the tiny kitchen's steaming mists
to windy heat, we scalded, peeled, and crammed
the countless acid cherries into jars
imprinted *Ball*. The radio softly jammed
Bruce Springsteen's "Born to Run," the bars,
hushed, revved the static air. Pregnant and sick
at forty-two, my mother cooled her face
with ice-hard cloths. Her room was hot and thick.
She slept. Those tomatoes kept us in place
that long July, learning the wifely art

of *putting up*. Red revolved in sealed glass;
the baby formed its blood and working heart.
We flailed our silent air guitars, the brass
clock ticked. Somewhere a Harley smoked the road.
On basement shelves, a few packed jars explode.

Ava Leavell Haymon

Four Eyes Gets Her First Warning

"One day," my Mi'ssippi uncle told me
"you gonna cross your eyes like that
and they'll stick." Said he knew
an ol man'd done it once too often
—I mighta seen him in town
down by the cotton gin.

The Leland boogeyman.
Shuffled back and forth forever
in slit-up shoes with squash-down heels.
One eyeball pointed over
accusing the other
that leaned clear out of its socket
to point right back.

Another pastime forbidden!
And I could do high, low,
or either eye at a time.
The sole entertainment allowed
during the sermon.

Dangerous habit, he was warning—
to tinker with the flat tableau
presented me, the world
gone double at my own command:
a forest twice as many trees,
black overlapping white,
preacher and pulpit making one voice
from two mouths, and
every tongue forked.

RED STARS-

Maggie Rosen

I Meet My Cat in Heaven and She is a Blonde

Her eyes have lost their slant,
but I know that keenness
even in this human form.
She still moves by pressing
on the pads of her feet,
still sits in windows,
angles her head to signal
I should comb her tawny hair.

She begins to talk,
and I realize it is
the same conversation we have always had.
Her back is to me,
and she tells me how she made room
for me in her heart
at great cost,
and I thank her.

I remark I am surprised
she made it up here,
after the mouse incident.
"Unfinished business," she says, stretching,
as she sashays
toward an angelic school of tuna.

Barrett Warner

First Out Are the Big Dark Bays

Their breathing is louder than their hooves,
the reins slapping their necks louder than breathing.
Five Eighths from the wire the riders set them down.
An old livered finger taps a watch and like reading
a book by moving our heads instead of our eyes,

we follow the horses' work with our faces,
sounding out the words like children—
a quarter in .22, galloping-out six in 1:10

A mighty blow, except the outside horse won't pull up.
Two outriders jog ahead to form a bottleneck, turning
and tightening as the runaway nears another quarter,
the dark-hearted panic louder than reins snapping.

Hours after my own trackers have gone out
and been put away, I can still hear an old love
shaking and sobbing at something gone awry.

David Sosnowski

Howard and Her

The scene through the keyhole is this:
the parlor with its piano, old books,
cushions, and Howard
and her,
in their eighties, sit (her)
and kneel (him)
atop the spread picnic blanket
where the two, once again,
are happily off
their lithium.

And the people from France aren't here,
can't come, have appointments
in heaven or hell,
one of those yellowing
black-and-white places.

Still, they wait
in their naphthalene, pinstripes, crinoline,
in their eyes and their skin
counting off the Mississippis
of this time exposure.

RED STARS-

The violin, pointedly,
is out of its case.

Strands of horse hair hang down
separately from the bow, as grey
as Howard's, as coarse as hers.
The Dixie riddle cups
where the wine was, sit,
one upright, a tower, the other,
an O, with a puddle of shine
at its mouth, rocking in the breeze
of a slowly rolling fan.

Cathryn Hankla

Ghost Family

A big welcome to the Ghost Family Reunion.
We only meet at funerals
In Holiday Inns south of the Mason-Dixon.

In little-used backwaters,
We blend into the scenic Blue Ridge Mountains
Or follow families with children to the Atlantic

As if we were a river winding to the coast.
But we are only a few sad reminders
Of the legions on the other side of the line:

Your sister, your husband, your aunt,
Uncle, cousin, mother, your father,
Your brother, your youngest child.

It's just a bad dream when we wake in cold,
Air-conditioned rooms, but our fashions
Confirm it: black stockings and black lapels,

A black boutonnière, for a touch of black humor.
If only this were prom night
And not a *danse macabre.*

So many gone now that it's a shock
To have one more funeral to attend.
It's like our own funeral after a while,

And we take issue with the hymns,
Start choosing our own and singing them
Instead. We want a jazz funeral, but then

Have to stop and wonder whether or not
We are really alive. And if we are not, what
Would it take to raise us from the dead?

And if we are still breathing,
What would it take to make us feel something
More than sad? Line us up and shoot

Our formal portrait. We're the Ghost Family Reunion,
The short living in front,
All the dead towering over us to the rear.

Moshe Dor

Lately Dead People

Lately dead people walk about
in my dreams. Sometimes
they are kin and sometimes

I don't know who they are, or
where they come from. They speak
the language of the dead, and grief

washes over me like lunar eddies.
They beg me to do something. Even
if I grasped what they wanted

I couldn't grant their wishes. *Please,*
I say. *Be patient. Maybe in time*
I will learn to understand, at least

to read your lips. But they go on
in their strange tongue until
they fade away, their eyes filled

with loss. When the alarm rings
I'm already up, clutching at my life
as it slips through my fingers.

Translated by Barbara Goldberg with the author

Richard Harteis

Tempus Fugit

for Tanya Grigorova Stoianova

I.

At my age
thirty years ago
he flew among
the stars alone
in a black sky.

Perhaps he heard
the crack of radio
communication, perhaps
not, he kept himself
entertained, on course,
and finally home.

II.

I see him
eating a sandwich,
master of the seamless
ocean, plotting his way
by constellation:
like poetry,
a lonely business

like perhaps his dysphagia
or whatever hard human thing
you can imagine,

singing alone
with a sandwich
among the stars.

Bina Goldfield

Stages

The winter landscape from the speeding train
is gaunt, miles of barren trees whose branches
are like stubble on an old man's face, scratchy
against a gray sky, which leads me to the
perennial bush clipped back each fall on my
father's grave that I visit each winter except I
missed this year which leads me to his stubble
before the Sabbath when the bathroom smelled
of sulphur from a lather he used because
an Orthodox Jew is forbidden to lay
a blade to his skin which leads me to
how he forgot the forbidden of the
taking of one's own life
which leads me to
he hanged himself clean shaven
which leads me to stare ahead
as the train pulls into the
dark tunnel leading me
to my station
stop

RED STARS---

Davi Walders

Requiem for Judith Resnick

"The world looks great." *J. R. from the space shuttle Discovery, 1984.*

Sometimes as though you were hovering,
as though you wished someone—anyone

to remember, I see you, a young girl
polishing her shoes, packing her lunch,

concentrating and deliberate, each choice
as serious as the dinner discussions,

Torah portion and algebra equations
that challenged you. Granddaughter

of a shochet, connected to ritual, family
and community, I see you, not here

on Bethesda streets walking among us
during your long years of preparation,

but far away, as in those one hundred
forty hours floating beyond the pull

of gravity or in dim, humming rooms,
just above charts and graphs, searching

green screens for red warning lights.
Pilot of your own fearless trajectory,

always the first to arrive, to board,
you are the first to settle into that

locked weightlessness, rising again
those last moments of lift-off, given

neither wings, nor chariot, nor chance
to fly too near the sun, leaving us

only the grace of a woman doing her
job and the dignity of your name,

that, too, eclipsed by others.

Ronald Wilson

Pentecost

Sun a pentecost
he speaks his tongues fire
in the divine wind
dancing so many to address
to praise he raises his palms
and caws full throated
beard intricate with knots
gift of times
gift of curving space
of velocity and purpose
this point around which
all things spin

Gary Lilley

Sanctuaries for the Deacon's Sons

This is the poem where my brother becomes
me in the pulpit at his Pentecostal church
and the faithful lean forward in their seats
as he witnesses having been a womanizer,
a liar, and a cocaine thief and how nothing
could touch him, how he'd laid on the side
of a lean shot glass until late in the day
with God over him, how he jack-hammered
holes in the crazy streets, bandana dripping
and him pushing the blade, how the summer
was the heat, and trouble and love simmered
to a circumstance, getting the sanctified strength
from the lockdown, proper shoes to walk parole,
the blues, Lucifer's night on the steel strings.

RED STARS--

Robert Krut

Inside the Heaven and Earth Machine

1.

Driving out of town, a flatbed with chicken cages
in front of me, white feathers lifting toward the windshield,
huge weightless snowflakes.

2.

Stop telling me we're God.
Just stop.
Already.
We're neither, and don't say it's in the details,
because the details here are this:

A snake shaking itself loose of the dirt pile,
working its way to our door, trailing
mud behind, forming a word in longhand.

3.

Mud drying, climbing your legs—
Your feet, buried in ground—
Screaming, the heat starts in your stomach,
Crawls in a pulse making all muscle, all vine.

4.

I know what you did while I was sleeping—
Nailed my feet to the surface of Mars, spun
The planet like a roulette wheel.
I raised my arms like a sail, collecting
Dust, stones within me as momentum built—

the sun, nothing more than a tiring star
breathing into a gaping mouth.

--1990-1995

Michael Waters

Parthenopi

Ios

Once we beheld the brilliance of our estate
reflected in the haloed serenity of the girl
who prepared the basketful of cucumbers for salad,
slicing each nub into watery wheels,
columns of coins in the egg-white bowl.
Then she'd lift each miniature transparency
as she'd seen the priest flourish the Host,
thumb the serrated blade
to nick the green, then twist her wrist
to peel back the dust-plumed skin, the rubbery shavings
heaping a wild garden, unspoiled Eden, on the wooden counter.
Again and again she consecrated each wafer.
We basked in her patience, that rapt transportation,
her bell-shaped, narrowing eyelids as she spun
one papery sun, then the next, her perfect happiness,
smoke from the blackened grillwork wreathing her hair,
the fat of the slaughtered lamb hissing in the fire.
Her name—we'd asked our waiter—was Parthenopi, "little virgin."
We were still a couple then, our summer's lazy
task to gather anecdotes toward one future,
each shared and touching particular
to be recited over baked brie and chilled chardonnay
in the grasp of some furious, if distant, winter.
"Parthenopi," one of us might say, chiming a glass,
but the common measure of love is loss.
The cucumbers glistened in oil and thyme.

Faye Moskowitz

Rainy Day in Vence

No stiff-legged promenade
on the Boulevard de Lattre
today...only a *danse macabre*
of clothes lines caught by

RED STARS--

rain. Trapped like damp
in stone walls, she curses
the husbandry that wouldn't
let her squander 40 francs
on six Red Emperors
blazing in a bowl...
Some folks *pray* for rain,
he says. The two: impatient
as guttering candles
waiting to go out.

Cathryn Hankla

How to Stop a Camel

The reins feel as insubstantial
As shoestrings slipping
Through the eyes of your hands.

You are riding blind with terror.
The humpbacked beast gallops,
A runaway train, car stalled

On the crossing. Hanging on
To its mane, you reach for one rein
And pull, training the force in a circle.

After the first dread and frothing,
The camel brakes, ever so slightly.
A few more swipes of this compass

Around a shrinking point, pinning
The tail, and your future loops
Your past, shooting out through

The present moment. The animal
Bows as you dismount.
Survival brings its own pleasures.

Michael Varga

A Camel-Trader's Gift

The half-blind man has only one eye, but he weeps just the same.
—Bantu Proverb

Hot beams curl 'round the horses' flanks,
bright arcs branded deep into the fly-buzzed flesh:
and as I tread afraid, a camel-trader sketches
a sign in the sand, prompting my gasp of thanks

that something human is here, something other
than the eyes of beaten bulls, tails swatting
seven times the pace of my slow steps over the rotten
bones of camels hacked in an earlier feast rougher

than you or I have ever witnessed. Glad to
shield my eyes from the flies and the heat, I crouch
beside him and stare below the turban at the pouch
bulging over his unseeing eye. Inside the pouch a few

suras of the Koran have been finely written to phrase
a reminder of his total submission to what Allah will,
to what Allah already wills—that he find his fill
of sights and cram them into a single eye's space.

His blood-crusted dagger paints the sand, his lips ashen,
my unlikely savior—I recall most his teardrops
slow-rolling in dusty streaks; story told, he stops,
both cheeks shimmer cleansed, that one eye acting.

Alicia Partnoy

End of the Millennium Latina

(a song)

If I'm murdered with the M, Montonera,
if I stumble into S, Sandinista,
will I somersault out of the alphabet—
if I come back in Z, Zapatista?

Hanging tight to the flag that's in love with me,
harvest of the land that provides for me,
caught on fire by the pain of each body
that suffers the spit flames of imperialism.

This year 2000 with its many zeros
is the end of some millennium and the start
of another struggle against being hollow,
an emptiness in history, a number on a list.

Translated by Gail Wronsky

Herbert S. Guggenheim

Pete Sussman Answers a Challenge from the Countess Lisa to Write a Sonnet in Less Than 24 Hours

"You're telling me that *you* know how to write
Elizabethan sonnets?
                                        Go ahead."
I didn't get an ounce of sleep last night.
I dragged myself to work today half dead.

For someone whom I've never hugged or kissed,
it wasn't easy writing on command.
But, after all, I'm such a narcissist.
And so are you!—your hair and face so planned—
your china face, your careful powder puff.

Yet, as coworkers, we can never touch.
And so I gulp down coffee, act aloof,
and focus on not liking you too much.

        I watch you disappear thin and serene—
        reflected in a chromium machine.

-1990-1995

William Heath

The Shining Path

Lima waits—under rat-gray
clouds that bear no rain—
for an invasion of babies.
In a shanty desert of tin
cans and cardboard they
sharpen their sexual weapons.
The night sighs with orgasmic
war cries. Babies are bombs.
At dawn a ragtag tide
seeps down the dry river bed
into the heart of the city,
submerging the market, the park,
the plaza of San Martin.
This is a hell no Virgil
could guide a poet across.
For every patch of street
there are two pistols
and the stale air is thick
with the sweaty smell of greed
you could cut like a cheese.
In the tree-shrouded suburbs,
in the homes of the rich,
from behind bougainvillea walls
crenellated with broken glass,
voices tinkle like lost bells.
A guard dog prowls every garden.
At dusk in the garbage dumps
children waltz over rotten fish.
As the moon rises they will follow
the shining path out to the razor's edge
where a chill wind blows, primes
bombs, and the cries of babies
soar up like flames.

RED STARS-

David Wolinsky

The "Three Laughers of the Tiger Ravine"

As if a line of optic fiber
connected here and distant China—
except the filament drops down a thousand years,
except that it shivers with silver fire,
and whirls back up from its autumn gorge
like a leafstorm drenched with fury of centuries,
to arrive as the ghostly voice of a laugher:
"Hello, Hello. Anybody at home or ill at ease
in their homebody? In history?
Chess anyone? Sassafras tea?"
"And where," you think eloquently
if not elegantly amid planted pines
"is the fury of centuries?" And here
your mistake. And roars the tiger.
And swaying bridge plunges. And of
the Three Laughers, their striped laughter.

ABOVE: Pat Hutchings reads at the podium while the audience in front row seats ponders her poem.

ABOVE, RIGHT: Toni Asante Lightfoot in 1996, and Askold Skalsky in 1997, reading under the stars.

LOWER RIGHT: Hilary Tham and Miles David Moore relax under their favorite tree before a reading in 1996.

III

"LET THE WHITE MOONS RIDE!"

—Joaquin Miller

P: Sydney March and George ung exchange views at a post-ding reception in 1997.

OVE: W. Perry Epes and Jacklyn tter smile after the 1999 Young ets reading.

POETS READING 1996-2001

ABOVE, FROM THE TOP: Michael Da[...] the Cabin's troubadour, serenades [...] the back porch, here in 1997.

CENTER: Patricia Gray prepares to read in 1998, as Jacklyn looks on.

BOTTOM: E. Ethelbert Miller honor[...] the young poets in 1999.

Roy Jacobstein

The Odd Morphology of Regret

Lint collector, abdominal eye, perpetual
seat of kindergarten curiosity——
insie or outsie?——

you reign: universally mammalian, very
center of our being, mute remnant
of Mom long after Mom's

become remnant, invaginated marker
of life's arc. (Insie and outsie
inexorably recede.)

But please, tell us, Señor Umbilicus,
Miss B. Button, why you lack
those *frissons* of feeling

that got us here, you who should be
the ultimate pleasure zone—
shapely, accessible,

clitoral, to whom reams of paeans
would certainly be penned—
why you remain so

utterly unerogenous, ghost port
where all the great vessels
once docked.

Linda Nemec Foster

Bad Art at the Clarkston Motor Inn

Insomnia lives here, right next
to the dust on the Gideon's Bible
forgotten in the night stand's
top drawer. So it's up 'til three

flicking through the static on the TV's
four channels, counting the mint
green tiles in the bathroom and
measuring the off-gray grout
that secures their universe.

Above the sink—a tiny mirror and
a tiny picture of an unmanned
sailboat floating in spite of itself
towards your reflection. And
back in the bedroom, stuck
on the wall near the closet
sits "The Old Sailor" thick
with acrylics and bad memory.
Is that a cloud or an afterthought?
How can a pipe resemble a nose?
Why does his disembodied face
loom like a storm on the horizon?

Forget him and look at what's
directly over the bed. The world's
largest pink carnations jumping out
of a too clear glass vase. Peering
down on your sleepless head,
they could be your last chance
for a little excitement. "Looks so
real you could eat 'em," the desk
clerk told you last night, extolling
the virtues of women and art
in the same room. Wide awake,
desperate, ready for anything.

Daniel Gutstein

Less and Less the Day's Happenstance

I'll call the tree *hourglass*—
a winter's deep soak, a spring of up-flow,
a summer's green thickening, and the leaves now fall.
Roots and limbs are each other's symmetry.

WHITE MOONS--

Tree in clay, tree in air. One drinks, one breathes.
I stand at my brother's grave.
No such connection here—
he is just as much fastening me to the ground
as my cheeks blush with his blood.

Then I'll say that bird is really red—
a ruby necklace of flight that flashes off
when the clasp breaks in the trunk's shadow.
A crisp, red drumbeat. So bright,
the tree will wear a dulling brown pelt
on a muddy shoe string...

A grave marker is marble for *who was here.*
The tree, its leaves falling to the last,
will represent itself. When I walk, the bird's flight
seems less and less the day's happenstance.
Either finery with a mind to circle the ephemeral
or vice-versa—the ephemeral with a mind.
How do I resemble the tree? I believe my eyes.
In moments when I look in the mirror,
my brother's thick lips turn my face handsome.

Gary Stein

Subway

When cities swell
with business, cramping
motion, men flow

through stone, pulsed
blood beneath skin.
The river parts

and we rattle the *Times*
in our fast seats, invisible
as a stranger's dream,

nodding on the aisle.
We lean toward each
stop as if with hope

while the train transfuses
itself. What enters
the heart enters between

beats. Above us doors
and faces wait to open
to our rising like flowers

dreaming. Sun blooms
over each stem at the same
deliberate speed. We

travel the winking lights
of the tunnel,
space between darkness.

Rose Solari

My Mother's Piano

What it must have cost her to carry that thing from rented apartment to rented apartment to rented house to the house they bought with the help of my father's GI bill to the house I grew up in—souvenir of her family's brief, mysterious period of prosperity, like my aunt's diamond ring, my mother's Wurlitzer baby-grand. Big as a boat. Glossy as patent-leather shoes. A literal-minded child, I worried that it, like other babies I had seen, was going to grow, and grow a lot, eventually squeezing us out of the living room, so that we'd spend most of our time in the cold, damp basement, or trapped in the narrow upstairs hall. If there's a god, I used to think, why is my mother so sad and mean? Why is her memory so bad that she remembers the B I got in geography but not the long, long list of A's?

But I was talking about the piano—how she would smile when she sat down to it, closing her eyes as if the music that rose from her hands had hands of its own that massaged her face. How her fingernails would click against the keys, a backbeat I thought was so impossibly adult, like face-powder or the bright red polish she'd said I wasn't ready for yet. "Three keys past an octave," she would boast, stretching her fingers out to show me the span of her hands, and I'd put my girl-palm up against hers to measure the difference.

OK, I think sometimes, so she could have been a teacher, a singer, even an actress; OK, I tell myself, she got a raw deal. She was still able, in the grace of the absence of words, to make something beautiful and good, her hands moving like light, like water over those keys. What came from her fingers then was a story, slow at first, and a little dark, speaking of generations who never had enough, and then of their children, and then of the fantasies that those children's children had—a curving staircase to walk down slowly, like Grace Kelly in a wide skirt, good light, smooth men with real jobs, real money, who knew their way with a cigarette lighter. Day to day my mother and I would be just two women who didn't know how not to hurt each other. But when she played, there was truce, always—her at her bench, me curled up on the rug beneath my mother's piano, both of us caught in the knowledge of all she'd never be.

Anne Caston

What Sings

Hot afternoons when we were twelve, to escape
the chronic *thou shalt nots* and the *go ye therefores*
of the godly people of our town, Verlene and I would drop
our heat-rank bodies into the swift, chill waters
of the St. John's and drift downriver half a mile or so
to where cypress grow out over the bank

in thick groves: we'd haul our bodies out, then upwards,
heaving ourselves into the muddy mouths of underwater caves.
When our eyes made sense of the dulled
light underground, we'd find ourselves
tangled among trees' roots which dangled
from the dark ceiling of the cave. We learned

a way to tip and slide our bodies, feet-first, into them.
Slung like that in the rough bark cradles, the watery
cave sparkling darkly around us, the lit and godly world
far-off and fading, we'd thread our fingers into the lacework
of smaller branches, pretending to be part of it—that
underworld where we were hung, two weary, dreamy children

drifting into sleep. Water lipped at the cave's mouth.
Far off: a barking dog, a horn. Church bells tolled the hour.
Somewhere our parents called to us. We slept
until the sun descended and the evening
trains wailed and thundered by,
our long sleep overturned then by the shuddering

earth over our heads. Under us, the tide was rising.
We shimmied free and slid our bodies
back into the wild current, swimming
upstream into the dying light, our hearts
thudding, and some dark thing in me starting to sing
a song like the song the miner's bird sings under the black earth.

Lola Haskins

Spell for a Poet Getting On

May your hipbones never die.
May you hear the ruckus of mountains
in the Kansas of your age, and when
you go deaf, may you go wildly deaf.

May the neighbors arrive, bringing entire aviaries.
When the last of your hair is gone, may families
lovelier than you can guess colonize
the balds of your head.

May your thumbstick grow leaves.
May the nipples of your breasts drip wine.
And when, leaning into the grass, you watch
the inky sun vanish into the flat page

of the sea, may you join your lawn chair,
each of you content
that nothing is wise forever.

WHITE MOONS--

Nathalie Anderson

Cold Sweat

Dangerous air, hot and cold at once,
chasing its tail through the azaleas.
Something sleek and vigorous, something
panting, shivery—fang in its mouth,
claw in its wing, sting in its tail: whip
in Persephone's dark bedroom. Like

meeting the one your old flame loves now—
no use in recalling how happy
you might have been. You're going to learn
to do without lushness, to do without
yawning roses. It's Colorado
vaporous at mid-day, Mojave

with the sun plunging: hot blood, cold heart,
air with a nip and a blister. You'll
learn from Shadrach, frost in the furnace.
No more gardenias. What we've got now
is chills and fever. The leaves turn up
their silver tongues. The wind says Ah.

Anne Harding Woodworth

Tintype 1890

When you pose for a tintype,
you enter into a keeping still, cold and thin.
A prop stiffens you at your neck,
lapels lie flat like a combed mustache.

Your legs cross with a sideways look,
and your hands settle on a thigh. Your eyes

show up brown on tin, yet they were blue,
and drying out, too, because

when you pose for a tintype,
you have your instructions to reach quiescence,
and when you want to close your lids against the light,
you can't.

Linda Nemec Foster

Nightmare

I'm the one with the madness
stuck in my throat, the dry lips
of the last man shot at dawn.
I'm the one you least expect
when the dream hatches in the room
like larvae changing into furniture,
ordinary chairs. I'm the man
perched on the ceiling, smooth
and far away. I'm the woman
with the painted lips bending
my mouth over rosary beads:
a string of skewered coal
I place around your neck.
I'm the deformed child
growing from your shoulder,
your shadow, the yellow
breath you exhale. I'm the fire
trapping you inside, your feet
the dusty floorboards that won't
move. I'm the scream that refuses
to leave your mouth and
your mouth a gaping hole
that redefines the idea of black.
I'm the murmur of gray walls,
the windows talking to themselves,

WHITE MOONS--

the mirror that cracks easily.
I'm the estranged lover with a knife
that cuts through your reflection
to reveal absolutely nothing.
I'm the fertile wound that keeps
bleeding, bleeding while the rest
of your life sits on its hands.

Linda Lee Harper

Imagining the Worst

presents no stretch of imagination.
Like a professional athlete warming up,
I know the signs before the day begins,
tightening bowels, muscle spasms,
aborted sit-ups, treadmill belt slipping
under my feet.

The milk sours on its way to my bowl.
Corn flakes, soft as flaccid jowls,
half-float, defy my spoon's swoops.
This bodes poorly, a bad day and I haven't left the house.
My tires, under-inflated, do not explode as I drive
over the speed-bumps, but the loose hubcap escapes,

hitting the neighbor's dog sharply enough to leave me
a vet's bill for $500 in my door later in the day.
Every lunatic on wheels follows or stops
my forward momentum and rain, no—a monsoon,
hovers over my windshield like a banshee.
Everywhere I hear sirens.

At work, all the students lie. They write
tiny absurdities even laughter won't dispel.
As their crimes mount, cheating seems
reasonable, leaving early, mandatory as breath.
One little girl, writing about an Edwardian wife gentle
as milkweed, unhappy as her husband is content,

says, "Mrs. Mallard was a genital wife whose husband
was probably very happy in their marriage," and in the margin
I write, *I should hope so,* hopelessly confusing the vocabulary-
challenged, my cynicism serrated as a carnivorous fish.
And going home, what wonders my cell-phone conveys:
a neighbor calling to say the fire company did what they could,

that I can stay with them as long as I want, them and their five
boys crafty as trolls, for as long as I'd like, for as long as I can stand.

Elizabeth Hazen

Tips from a Nude Model

If you sit still long enough, your ass can fall
asleep; the loss of sensation is gradual,
like an erasure. Never be afraid
if you cease to feel, as long as you get paid.
Once, my entire arm awoke to pins
and needles pricking through my toughened skin,
but I stayed still until the timer rang,
unfurled my body and when the burning pang
subsided, finally I felt nothing sharp
or numb. I strummed the air as I would a harp
with my left hand; my right hand fisted, punched
my leg from knee to toe. My knuckles crunched,
blushing with impact against my frozen feet
that took each blow as thick gray cuts of meat.

When you resume the pose, your torso cast
across your lap, the students stare, amassed
like children at the zoo. They see your skin
as a mixture of complements and you begin
to feel frantic inside yourself; eyes swing
like pendulums across the studio, urging
the minutes on. Never let anyone
touch you and never laugh. When you are done,

WHITE MOONS--

get dressed, collect your pay, but never smile.
Know that your body may be numb awhile.
As you see yourself reflected in the paint
observe the color and ignore the faint
glimmer he put in your eye that isn't you.
Forget who you are, the nothing that you do.

Rod Jellema

Think Narrow

One of six million rods or cones
in the eye will flash one cell
of the billion in the brain
at the end of the thread of optic nerve
to catch a single ray from a streetlight
as it bounces off black water
asleep in a pothole.

This predicts the way the stem
of a coconut palm
leans long and far away
into pinpoints of light we call stars.
Come dawn, a split second of music
in the thin sing of a finch
will slip into the crack between two notes
the way a tiny lizard darted just now
into a slit in the garden wall.

Think narrow. Think the line of light
that leaped under the bedroom door
to save the frightened child who was you.
Your thin escape from being someone else.
The slender grace
of a sudden thought that takes you
past your self, walking

the good gray heavy town,
the bulge and muscle and long bone

that enables a wisp of thought to walk
these streets, themselves created by thought.
Think how we stride the wide earth
pressing down our weight and our love,
exulting in the plump swell of growth,
knowing the narrow gift of incarnality
is ours by the skin of our teeth.

M. L. Liebler

A Lonely Blues To Be

for Andrei, Brigitte, Laura and Sally in the Alley
French Quarter, New Orleans, 2001

Her heart is a globe
With hidden places that
Could end the slavery
Of this mortal coiled world.

She knew things
That were deeper
Than the muddy waters
Of the Mississippi Delta.

"There are some secrets," she said,
"In this world that can't be
Kept inside too long
Before the Southern river sun
Dances them out from under
The leaves of our humid lives."

So, we are left to shake our mysteries
Like Voodoo rain sticks only to find
Stones have settled one atop the other to build
High walls around our broken luck selves.

She's my Tarot, tea leaf,
Good omen of luck lying—
Waiting for me back in

WHITE MOONS: ·

The dark swampy bayous of the delta
Where I listen to the mud singing
Me to sleep—a lonely blues played
Against the face of the rising sun.

Sydney March

The Summer You Said "Yes" To Me

I no longer yearn for beaches
now I pluck imaginary seagrapes from
your breasts and your cheeks become mangoes
sweetened by lethargic days.
That summer the chronic boredom of summers
vanished in your tangled geography of dance
and the surf-song of your voice
rode the air in madness.

There were no beaches
no coconut trees that summer of your arrival
the fickle flowers of spring had vanished
as swiftly and silently as they came.
Summer burst upon the scene, a conjurer
offering dreams, promising gifts.
I dreamed landscapes of mangoes,
plums, enormous palms
crowned with Zulu headdresses.
The bearded sun of childhood seared my face
until my nostalgia for bougainvilleas
and pale sandy beaches became clouded
by the automobile fumes.

It was that summer I watched you dance
whirling rain forests of rhythms
tossing the seasons off your body.

Miles David Moore

Duck Stamps

The way I'm living now is like when you're at the post office,
and you need stamps desperately, but want a beautiful design
to give your correspondence some putative distinction,
but the clerk at the counter is out of the first six designs you ask for,
and you want to see the stamps she *does* have, but it's almost lunchtime
and she looks as if she keeps a gun behind the counter,
and there are nineteen people behind you, each with a package to mail,
and they all look as if they keep guns under their coats,
so you tell the clerk you'll take anything, and she gives you a book of duck
stamps,
twenty green mallards pointing their bills stiffly to the left,
decoy eyes stuck square in their heads, seeing nothing, making contact with
nothing,
lined up like a shooting gallery for disgruntled postal clerks,
and you feel every bit as wooden and lifeless as the ducks
as you paste them on the envelopes of twenty past-due bills,
while others emblazon love letters with pictures of movie stars,
and great events of history, and every flower of the field.

Sharon Negri

What She Did

From the start
Mother taught me to shop for bargains
mid-60's Market Street, Blake's department store,
Friday nights we headed straight
for sale tables in Clothing.

Today, I am one in a city of one-half million,
dutifully searching Macy's half-off rack,
do the math in my head,
check purity of fabric next: silk, cotton, linen,

WHITE MOONS-

my fingers have learned
to distinguish 100% from blends,
though she warned early about expectation:

even when you press you will rarely be successful.

Amid the just-reduced slacks,
I recall her lessons on fit, how there is no substitute
for correct proportion and

with a small size, choices will be limited.

I browse clearance skirts last,
having memorized the rule: if summer whites
are not lined, a slip must be worn,

one's shape should never be exposed by light.

Could she have imagined then
I would pay full price for a linen dress and plan
to let it wrinkle as it wills, give myself up
to the whims of its thinness and weave?
When I wear it, she'll no doubt say
looks like you slept in it.
I'll cradle her hands, reply yes,
and I will keep dreaming
wildly through my day because of it.

Michael Reinke

Mother

How the memory chooses me, time after time.
        How it haunts that at last we've stopped, without
Alternatives, at the Maryland bank of the river, federal
        And famous, the road appearing to end

Or emerge from a mirror grave and mansed
        As an affair of State— and the ferry,

-1996-2001

White on the hour, filling, half-filled, shaded
        With people who not even looking at you beckon,

Waits— and then you rise, refusing my hand,
        Completely taken over with the boat
Elegiac, in its slip, the preparations, and soon
        The actual event of departure, swan-like, overly

Elegant, a master gesture given by a minor
        God. I will notice, in this tableau of separation
Arrangement, distance, placement— and then, a son's
        Preoccupations: the yet reached shore, the boat

Moving, and to this day, not forgotten, your own
        Step forward. All the light reeling as absence.

Martha Sanchez-Lowery

Marking the River

School is a river
daydreaming out of tall windows
a cross-eyed watch of the silver flowing still
your mother thought you a little slow
but learning was a wild place
on the river's edge
where you set feasts of honeysuckle
on broad green leaves
'til they called you in late from recess
back to the mapmaking, the charting and intoning of river thought
then the run home in the river making rain
hail and thunder defiant
watching the river making
what ran between the cobblestones
late
and much later
there is
spring snow

petal pink
drifting on the road
borders of shameless color
sloping away
from the embankments
and the river is now marked
by wires, silver flags
marked for a river race
and it is a known place
you could mark yourself
in that same way
single scull cutting the water
so close to the mark
and going forward faster
than the river itself

Askold Skalsky

Schumann's Finger

If one could sum up all the rest,
it would be the third, the devil's finger.
Fourteen days devoted to one étude
and still the dry, cold keys, everything
too slow for virtuosic strength.
I need an apparatus of the century,
translating impatience into consummation,
binding the index finger into swaddling clothes,
like a tight cigar, so that the middle one,
the orphan, strengthens, nature gets a boost
commensurate with what can yet be done.

It doesn't matter in what form,
pain too can be attractive. I sketch it
in A major; ten days afterward it fails,
the finger gone completely mad,
rigid like a tiny corpse. The *medicus*
says baths in bovine extracts will suffice,

but what if they rub off on more than just
the stiff topography of my poor hand?

I play the piano rarely now (who wants
to be like Liszt anyway) and can compose
without it just as well. Sometimes
when the music stumbles out, wanting
to pound the breath before it, supple,
like a panting hammer, I ask God,
Why this? and face October the only way
I can, moving from the fourth floor to the first,
where it's only a short distance
between the window and the street below.

Terence Winch

The Deal

I'm afraid to tell you what I'm really like.
When I see birds I think of disappearances
and cold times when you can't get warm
no matter what, and when I am surrounded
by computers, I drift off into the gap between
now and never, and I float there, lost to all.
At work I am a prisoner of the present
moment, which cracks over me
in a series of disastrous temptations.

I am reluctant to reveal the way my body
knows the correct answers to my problems,
because I told my parents I would keep
the secrets of their lost realm. But I can say
that desire and despair are faint messages
I hear always and can't tell apart.

I am too embarrassed to speak plainly
about my childhood, which came and went
without looking, without seeing, without
knowing. I embraced the future like a fish

learning to swim, so today faces in photos
watch me like golden birds on the tree
of attachment, and the laws I live by
are written on the backs of recipes.
Something beautiful may happen yet,
and teachers may appear, but time
is the money that runs out just
when you're wise enough to spend it.

Elizabeth Rees

Waiting

Standing on my back porch
under shadows of the trees,
I watch the sky sweep
fog along and think of first
offerings: the effort of my body,
mind in body, moving, shifting
eggs from side to side.

I won't know where color comes from
or why these rust unfurlings
keep time like a clock. I reach
over the railing, I move from foot
to foot. My uterus tugs.
The wind scatters milkweed
because the wind is a seed.

I imagine hundreds of women
leaning over their porch railings,
something in them releasing, tilting,
as the moon contracts. My back yard
changes color in its case.
How many eggs will we offer?
How many hands will wait?

Nancy Naomi Carlson

What Cannot Be Held

I might have called her *Chayala* for life,
but knew her only as shadow and light,

an echo on a sonogram screen,
a preview of a chord I'd never hear.

Her image was gathered from swipes of a probe.
Sifting through layers of tissue and bone,

the trained eye could pick out from fluid's play
the outline of heart and head, digits that waved

like sea anemones. Different views—
cross-sectional maps—guided the search for clues

to the flaw, knitted in code and handed down
the line. Figure rose from changing ground,

hovered ghost-like and then, reversing roles,
broke up into static that would not hold.

Andrea Collins

After the Second Night of Your First Ob/Gyn Rotation

You said you knew your mind had drifted from feeling
for the landmark you knew, the low womb of your young patients
too poor to go private so help's your rookie hands,
to our daughter, and birth's warm pigment, blood,
momentarily muffling a newborn's lush cry
or coating the vague stare of a newborn

WHITE MOONS---

when suddenly you plunged, almost elbow deep
you insisted over dinner, over Sesame, over the night sky,
consumed by a blank pouch, a hysterectomy.

You had no idea how deep you'd go. Tonight
as you feigned sleep in the center of our bed
where our baby sometimes sleeps, and as I imagined

I was that pounding heart failing to burst your chest,
you pushed me, deliberate, I know, far to the edge of the bed.

Joseph A. Davis

Fat Tuesday

You tap-danced over
to greet me, teased
my eye-tips as the
Burgundy evening glowered.
You touched me, faithful
as a snake-handler,
and we ate the night
like starving dogs,
tossed our personal
security into the crowd,
wasted no more day-
time on innocence,
fire-walked across
the busy street,
swam into swagger
and chanky-chank,
blind-sided by crying
accordion smiles.
We shuffled on the
dusty snakeskin floor,
wonder-drunk
to the soles
of our shoes.

--1996-2001

Lola Haskins

How I Learned

for D'Arcy

For years I made you purple presents.
Mauve blouses, lavender skirts,
fuschia scarves that flowed.
For each occasion, another shade
of bruise, sweet as the fumes of
Daddy's disappearing Buick, achy as
the strokes of tight-lipped Mommy,
brushing my hair. I thought you'd
wear them. I thought they'd become
you, being blonde. But you put them,
all my purple gifts, in one deep drawer.
And now, grown, you take them out.
At first it pains, how new they are.
Then you smile. *Let's give these*
away, you say. And the spring sun
back-lights your hair. You look
like some kind of angel, standing
there in your bedroom, the shine
of what to keep, and what to let go
falling through both our hands.

Wendell Hawken

Winter Scene at Evening Stables

Let's say, five o'clock in mid-December. You're down
at evening stables, your quilted Carhartt's on.
The bare brown hills roll pink with color
borrowed from tomorrow and white's in every word
you mumble to the dogs. Your neighbor's barn's
a line of yellow squares, as yours must shine for her.
She's younger than you, has yet to get her horses in.

WHITE MOONS--

You've herring-boned your stone dust aisle.
Each halter on its hook, water buckets full
rakes and pitchforks put away, you've had your whiff
of summer in the open bales of clover and alfalfa hay.
Your horses have that look they get—thoughtful, far away—
chewing grain. Oh, sure, you think about Tahiti
or living life one wall away from other lives.
How it is to take your coffee back to bed
and read till nine. But then you'd have to lock the house
and always piss inside. You'd weed and mow
for stranger's eyes. God knows what all.

Halfway up the hill, the dogs turn and wait.
Your neighbor leads two horses in
as yours stand deep in appetite. Their slopes of neck and rump
and counter-curving spines gleam under yellow light.
Another ordinary day. You flip the switch and shut the door.
Whatever ordinary means.

Rod Jellema

Ice Age

(Circa 1932)

for Robert Burton

The wet brown canvas
that covers the load of ice
smells like mushrooms sour
under blackening leaves
deep in a woods.
But with one heave the iceman
peels it back
and flings open his kingdom
to August daylight.

The shine of his pick
cracks ahead of its point
down seams of the ice blocks,
it splits open ravines and valleys

as he showers meteors skyward
in a spray of rainbow cold.

Some days he'd toss us crystal
shards as we watched from the curb.
With a *chunk* of the tongs
he'd heft a block of ice
high onto the blue of his shoulder
darkened to black by water.

It comes back, that ache
through the teeth while staring at ice,
waking up the dreamed geographies
between the spin of star-ice in space
and the warm tar paving of home—

a world, the shakes
of an idling truck, a stain
that spreads, two boys and a dog,
a rusted ice pick calling
far down in a drawer.

Brandon D. Johnson

Still Ain't

look. a man's head is not to be looked into by a woman
as if you could understand what you were seeing
since most of what we're thinking we don't
know why we're thinking it anyway. Like now.
I'm looking at the feet of the woman
in the white sandals at the next table whose
aged legs don't meet up to any standard
I'm aware of, but her feet, her feet are
attractive in a bony, bulging vessels sort
of way, and I'm guessing that the old guy
with her must be attracted to her feet
her feet at the end of those mediocre legs.

WHITE MOONS--

I'm sure you'd have a hard time understanding
why I'd find her feet anything worth staring at, as you try
to trace the bead of my eyes to figure out
what's going on inside my head.
you'd think I'm some foot fetishist if you knew
because that's probably on your mind every time
you writhe on the bed while I suck your toe
like the first popsicle of a ninety degree DC day.
But, maybe you're not thinking that at all.
I mean, if you're able to assemble that kind of thought
while every nerve in tongue's-reach is being detonated
firing like one spark plug trying to run a twelve cylinder engine
your face contorted as if I was grinding my heels into your feet
your feet fighting to get away from my pit bull lip grip
your big toe going deeper into my mouth while your hands feebly try
to cover your face like playing peek-a-boo with a kid on a bus
if you can keep track of your head while all that's going on
when all I can do is look at you and get aroused, try to keep
control of your foot
your foot that I love so much, then
maybe looking into my head wouldn't be so difficult for you after all
but ***you still ain't*** gonna figure out exactly what I'm thinking.

Vladimir Levchev

A Mason

I built my home on a strong rock—
on the sky.
Stones thrown at me
would reach me
only if they became birds.

The trees in front of my home
are tall-stemmed rainfalls.
I gather the fruit:
July thunderbolts.

Those clouds I travel in
are changing continents
that breathe in a world ocean.

The sun is my bright grave.
The moon is a secret face in my dream.
My tongue is my home
on a rock...

So, my arguments are well-grounded:
I based myself on the sky.

Toni Asante Lightfoot

What Girls Learn From Women

for Edith, Lynn, Kim, Karen & Yvette

she waited with her four girls
for him to come home
after a while Nina Simone
escorted Billie Holiday
to the turntable
love me or leave me
don't explain warbled from their lips
as southern comfort spilled
for the sisters who've been here
by dawn he'd arrived
his talk as sweet and putrid
as the leftover perfume
on his shirt

maybe he enchanted like Sam Cook
or begged like The Temptations
who knows what trick of language
he mastered in the years of doing this dance
some women flit like moths

WHITE MOONS-

toward flaming tongues
daughters wonder
why must we witness
our mother going up in smoke?

M. A. Schaffner

Gutters Cleaned

You can see everything and it all makes sense:
one of the lost Dead Sea scrolls holds up a part
of the roof weakened by terrorists; the work of
generations of naively ambitious swallows
tumors the soffits. And this is just

what lies before you. Over an aching shoulder
interesting cavalcades of runners
shuffle under sporadic shade. Windows open
as if frozen in mid-gasp, the pale curtains
teased by a wind returning the exhalations

of previous summers. If we have greater storms
we can blame leaf blowers and our own tendency
to laugh out of doors. Meanwhile, this job to do:
picking perfectly ordinary objects from where
they have no need to be, grooming the domicile

like a bird on a friendly rhinoceros, its wings
used only in case of death. I have no truck with
the usual angels, only the stay-at-homes who vie
for the smallest spots on the pin head on which
to chance a private fandango. Like flying squirrels,

there are more of them than you would think, sleeping
where you'd least expect them during the day
then coming out at night for the rumored party—
straddling gables or sipping from where the roof sags
and the moon rests, as if you had drawn it a bath.

-1996-2001

Thandiwe Shiphrah

There Are Curse Words In This Poem

I'm sitting at the bar of Boston Seafood—the last place in this city
where you can have a cup of coffee and a cigarette
at the same time.

A woman enters and seats herself to my left.
She is smoking a Benson & Hedges Ultra Light Menthol.

So am I.

We survey the menu. When I decide what I want
she crushes her cigarette and orders the same thing.
I turn to greet her but then she rolls her eyes toward
the back of her head and begins to yell at no one I can see.

Crazy, I think.

I revisit the menu, wondering what it's like
to be so tight with yourself that the two of you
can settle an old argument

in public

without caring whether anybody overhears.

Mary-Sherman Willis

Iron

My brute steam iron does
violence to your shirts, spurts and hisses
from its silver cheeks and its searing face,
(its red eye shimmers when it's on—hot!)
to make the sharp collar fold I like to kiss,
sharp as a blade,
when you say goodbye.

WHITE MOONS--

The wrinkle-breaker charts a course
across latitudes of cloth, circum-
navigating from your heart, away, across
the back you'll never see,
the dark side, its twin pleats, plumb
lines at your shoulders,
on to nose around the buttons

you will fasten one by one,
starting at the throat. Creases sealed
along the sleeves run to the cuffs,
and your shirt submits to me,
the St. George of order, with my sword,
this bloody iron, navigator through your
disarray, my compass, my love.

George Young

The Sweetness Of Disordered Air

Wyoming, there is nothing out there
except clouds

Driving north to Sheridan, you and I, the sky
just shy of crushing us,

we gradually become aware
that Plato must have been wrong.

For there are violet bruises, pearly bosses, dark hugs
and streamers of white silk. But how

could there ever be
a single template for a cloud?

Mist shapes itself in the empty sky
without a plan. Clouds

are born, clouds hurry, clouds die. It seems God
does play dice with the universe.

When the rain starts
squirming on the windshield, you peel an orange.

I pop a wedge in my mouth, open the window
to spit out a pip. And suddenly

we are splashed
by the delicious wet air of Wyoming.

Jane Alberdeston

out of body

a thief
I slip through your window
over the sleeping shadow of her body
and steal you away—

over rooms of grass that marimba
with the memory of lovemaking,
into beds of banana leaves slick with mist,
down streets black with frustration,
cutting the air with the sickle of my wanting,
starting a riot with your laughter,
weaving like smoke
through the kinky strands of my hair—

airports know me by the echo in my teardrops
and swear your love is luggage they'll never find

a dizzy gnat around fruit, circling the globe
while you search lost cities for metaphors

But it is fine—for now—
to measure the day by the harbor light
of your voice, to hold your words like wishing stones,
pocket them as if they wore the eons of the earth,
polished by sea kisses,
humming with the motion of my hips

WHITE MOONS-

A midnight marauder,
I leave you home again
(my fingers blue weeds pressed to the cool pane)
a remnant of nightfall in her hands, sleepily
touching your chin,
a muted oath in the gray curls of your beard
still burning from our journey
like a comet's tail.

Holly Bass

gleam

I am genetically predisposed
to be a domestic

like my grandmother
and her mother

I am not a domestic
I am not even a tidy woman

In my own home, I only clean
when absolutely necessary
Yet I walk into public bathrooms
and begin to clean the toilets

After I wash my hands, I wipe
the sink dry and
keep drying
until a whole row
of sinks gleam

I can't help myself
In restaurants, I clear crumbs from
the table of people sitting next to me
before the waiters have a chance

I do not accept tips
In bathrooms, I sing a happy
song while I work
I do this when no one is looking
I do this for the sheer joy of cleaning
that which does not belong to me

I do not know why I still do this

Rick Cannon

Point of Arrival

He stands barefoot on the gray concrete,
the iron season cooling the blood
dull red through his flat slow soles.
He's forgotten why he came to the garage
and stands in his shaggy robe before hammer,
awl, and ratchet, dumb, blank,
as if stunned by a piece of news.

Out the window he sees
the tight copse of trees—stripped
spar and mast—shrouding
in pale yards of light.

Still he stands, lost,
but beginning perhaps to sense, as dawn
will seep beneath a blind, that from far away
and through much trial he's come
exactly here. And as he stands, issuing

breath, the slow rhythm leaf by leaf,
he feels the earth shift slightly
under tonnage of wind
toward white winter.

WHITE MOONS-

For several minutes, he stays his feet
flat on the stinging stone,
a robed man in a cold garage
accepting his extremity,
seeing it had always been so:
even from the beginning he'd been,
by far, out too far to survive
more than just this little while.

David Gewanter

Chai 1924-2000

for Yehuda Amichai

Page of sand, scab-flakes of ink;

page of sand, page of skin:
where are you now?

On the tongue, life is a verb
and death, a proverb:
Apple eats apple-blossom,

seed eats the apple....
Your name, in the macaroni
of tongues, Ah-me-*hide,*
foreign and sentimental

as the pendant *Chai*—life—
noosing the ancients of St. Pete
waiting for the Early Bird Special

—or the girls in Bolinas
you saw loosening

their tefillin-strap

bikinis: souls
opening and closing,

a prayer drifting everywhere
but up—
Proverbial waves lap

a beach of crumbs.
Letters swirl in fat broth,
a name is lifted to the lips;
waiters wipe

the clock face clean.
Drop the page,
come out. *Come out:*

the body is an apple
to the seed,

the body is a seed in the earth.

Sean Enright

Anger

At first glance into my fire I saw the wood was winning.
The yellow flames larked about the squatting log,
dignified and toadish, unfeeling, blacker than solace,
not at all like the guy who would be last to leave the party.
But fire seemed a thing wood tolerated, barely.

I was not famous. Soon my son would be able to say
the word *famous*, he could already say *anger* and he
wasn't even two. (Matter of fact, he said it all the time.)
He would be famous for saying *famous* so young,
and I'd be his old da, fire-watcher, old mess-in-the-head.

In 1862 alone Emily Dickinson wrote 366 poems.
In each one something of the sticky silk she cast
for 24 hours caught, and then you felt her eating her web

WHITE MOONS--

like a barn-spider. She'd blow on the ink and sew the poem
into the year's packet, on top of yesterday, toss it in a drawer.

I'll bet in her whole life Dickinson never tossed a thing.
In her first poem that year, *wearing the sod gown,*
she rode out to meet her male friend, the End.
Useless feeling burning slowly inside out,
fire rasping, new flames spread thin like a father,

no longer to stand in the maw of the hungry beast of self
and crack a joke about it, as now the flames laid low
suddenly red as if with my son's *anger*, picking their teeth,
stuffed with tree pieces under the grate, like fish spines
picked clean of what they thought they were about.

At least it solaces to know that there exists—a Gold—
her standard undecayed. But even gold burned
in my fire: the blazing brass fire-dogs panted,
the rain sang in the burning dead branches
of the sugar maple, the rain sang for its life.

Michelle Gil-Montero

The Tub

As water is said to persist:
bent opal we call a current
with a coyote skull in his hands

summons another body
spits ink through an eye hollow

rolls his oars
like penciled gridlines on a lithograph

Could have collapsed there
in the tub

under the window
where the sun cuts in
linearly through the bamboo blinds

and now late August   in the dry air
recognized myself on paper
as in pocket of bone

Patricia Gray

Blackberry Bushes

take root where the soil is poor—
bloom on leached earth,
sprout past abandoned cars
and broken glass, like this love
growing past marriages
gone vacant with ruin.

The sweet fruit shows up late:
succulent, inky, buzzing
with juice. Pickers brave
thorns—pull back hooked
hands bleeding and scratched.

Wounded, they vow, "Never
again," but some plump nectar
draws them to the bittersweet
last-of-the-summer temptation—
juicy, teeming with growth.

WHITE MOONS-

Roy Jacobstein

La Création

—Chagall Museum, Nice

for Linda

Naked, from out the blue vortex,
a grown man lightly borne
in a blue-winged angel's arms
bends his head to the staggering light,
a man newly born, looking
to the world above, the world
of fish and the yellow moon
and the woman curved like a giant red ear,
the red sun, swirling, blown
out of an angel's horn,
the ram-headed man with the red Torah,
the shtetl, the rabbi, the ladder,
the menorah's nine lemony flames,
the purple-breasted women,
the blue lyre held by the blue king,
the donkey, lion, goat,
the golden fish with hands for fins,
the bearded butterfly. Above,
above His Son swaying on the white Cross,
flaccid abdomen covered at the groin
by a gray-fringed prayer shawl,
above it all, disembodied, two hands,
the visible hands of hiding
God, proffer twin tablets shaped
like pale loaves, or gravestones,
and I put my arm around my new wife's waist,
and she puts her arm around mine,
and we hold like that a minute
in that white room, in that white light,
infinite wavelets of white light.

--1996-2001

Ann Rae Jonas

Stroke by Stroke

Carrying food, tools, field notes, gifts of seed and iron
for Indians they met along the way; long days spent
scanning the horizon for storms, attending to hunger and
thirst, to sweat-soaked clothes and muscles growing strong;

the rhythm of rowing a background to thought, to talk of
God and how they'd save the Indians—counting paddle
strokes, the Jesuits made their way around Lake Superior
and drew a map, the finest for 150 years.

The goal was not the usual one of a journey: to cover distance
and arrive. Nor was it simply to count: sacks of provisions emptied,
paddles worn and lost. They did count strokes—work itself
was the unit of measure—but through the measured wake,
the Jesuits earned the revelation of shape.

Michael Reis

The Wiffle Specialist

I am a wiffle specialist.
I lower the chair for long kids
and raise it up for short ones.

Any kind of kid,
I clip his head close
and sooner or later
the ears make him angry.
He pays and slams out of here
and they stick out like dishbowls.
And each one is touchy and bulging
and looks like it could get Katmandu
if the lobe wiggled.

WHITE MOONS--

But I am a wiffle specialist.
I satisfy fathers.
I make
little enemies.

Amy Jo Ross

Overlook, Washington, D.C.

Michelle, it is late October and the leaves
are lonely and dirty—smelling like cheap rum
and semen, clustering under park benches,
so that now, wind clutching my sleeve, I am no
closer and you are much further than before.
What I remember, Michelle, is the sky's slow
sickness sifting over the fountains and you
standing parallel to the trees, tricking me
like fever. Faintly, only faintly, crickets
come, their wings opened or rubbing together,
mirroring my hands, thrusting darker, deeper
and, Michelle, we lie symmetrical for once.
This is the city you loved most, with its first
sex and intimacy like cherry blossoms
spread out over monuments and cathedrals
each spring. This is the city I've tried loving
again and again, with its male prostitutes
and politicians and dull, dreary winters
dissolving like darts in dingy bars. So when
I rushed home, twilight, against the rats, you laughed,
and boiled apples into mulled wine. We did not
speak. We hoped the wet, sickly bark of a dog
like dim starlight or the whimpering sunlight
slipping over the hospital would remind
us. Here, we make master's degrees instead of
babies, bent on some trailer park memory
with cracked mirrors and rust stains in the toilet
and it is enough, Michelle, to share our soiled
maternity dresses and dream of cities.

-1996-2001

Robert Sargent

Things That Go On Between Us

Standing at the elevator, you are saying
I don't have to go with you, down to your car.
But I say, "Who knows what might happen—
Someone may get on the elevator, I might say
Something about this person, walking to your car.
Then you might say something back,
An observation spoken with loving profundity,
Something that shows me again the depths of your heart.
I don't want to miss that."

Angie Blake-Moore

Missing

One short year later, the tattoo
of the American eagle I had etched
into my backside has flown the coop—
leaving a scant trail of patriotic ink, dotted
here and there like Hansel's bread crumbs.
My skin a map of treacly streaks, the remnants
of a poorly fought civil war. The eagle used to grip
a banner that read, "Don't Tread On Me."
Now it says, "o ea O e." The missing
letters have slid down my back,
an avalanche of typography. They rest
somewhere in the folds of my ass, my
lover reports. I have to take his word for it—
contortions in the mirror show me little. The light
is bad and I am misty-eyed. The tattoo
has melted away like lipstick, like newspaper
left out in the rain—the colors of the Sunday
funnies floating on the skin of the sidewalk.
There is just enough left to guess at the word balloons,
to fumble for the right punch lines.

Myra Shapiro

The Wind

There's nothing sexier than summer
wind sailing through a screen

so that I put my book aside to let it love me.
Today it came, an unexpected

riffling through the branches of a hickory tree, unexpected
since nothing moves

in Tennessee in mid-July; dead heat
lifts only for a storm

flashing—a moment—leaving not this breeze
but air that's lead, not this

gaiety spilling seeds through the magnolia leaves.
Of course I dropped my book—

such luxury in motion, mingling heat
and gentleness teased me

to make love to myself, which is delicious—

but then Paolo and Francesca
flew into my head, lovers Dante visits early

in a hell that's hardly hell and yet
it is, hot wind they'll forever circle in, hearts bound

by what they read, to longing, to a kiss,
to you, dear Dante, coming here yourself to hand

me warning, to lift my nose
out of a book and walk me past the porch, the open window.

-1996-2001

Nathalie Anderson

Juke Box Memories

Just another couple making juke box memories
And walking into trouble hand in hand.
—Terry Allen

He used to play ball. Now he works the rodeo.
He has one question: what do you do for fun?

He asks every woman at the bar. I don't have the answers.
I read. I go to the movies. He keeps his eyes shut when he dances.

I'm a real lady, he tells my friends at the table. It's not an insult.
There's no doubleness in him, not like Cathy

her mouth closed on his tongue on the dance floor.
She reads too, but she won't say so.

He wants to work construction, he's that steady.
His hand's hot on my hip. He never moves it,

never insinuates himself. Take it
or leave it. Cathy does both. I believe

he's never seen me. He doesn't know my name.
He calls me honey. "Honey," he says

"just because it's dark
don't mean I'm not looking."

Patricia Davis

After Reading of Dante's Ascent

I've come from the place
without light, where like you I wandered
in exile, tapping the ground, knocking against the edge

WHITE MOONS-

of my bones. I hoped I might be
the shell of an egg, I rapped the dome
of the sky overhead.

Sanza speme vivemo in disio.

I am neither round like an egg,
nor hard nor fragile
nor winged nor seething with snakes.

You teach me of skin
unhindered by feathers,
shoulders unburdened by wings.

Sean Enright

Spiderman

Death is outer space come down to earth.
Picking blackberries once on a hot green hill
we saw a yellow orb-weaver spider
put a zig-zag stitch in the bottom of its web.
A swell of happiness. But that night
you cried out crisply and when I looked in
you took a deep breath *here we go*
arching your back showing me where.
Feel my back, daddy.

You will not remember my sweetest season,
but I will tell this story again, my music,
my perfect condition, about one thing alone,
there's no turning away from your melody
as one can get stuck on a line of a poem,
which wants to be music but is only *to* music,
as this is about you and to you.
Someday they will also lap at you,
the low tides of mystery,

absent outdoor commands, furious black seasons,
the laughed-off infinite of foggy nights,
a moon yawing in a mist. Above, the branches
are coming for you like forks, like bare arms.
Nothing important moves for miles.

A light year is shorter than knowing a soul is gone.
Pressed to this instant, the heart hurt like a stopped fist,
my hand steady on you, little lazy god of work.
My boy, my love, my truly poem, I will hang
head-down in my garden web even when I'm gone into space,
at rest in the cords of creation, marvelous stuff,
stronger than steel, only fused quartz is stronger
than spider silk. And if the web should break?
Trap-door and recluse spiders, wandering and fishing spiders,
we'll all pour down like silver and start again.

W. Perry Epes

Black Fire

Poring over the contour map
of somewhere out West—slopes of gulches
where leaping flame can far outrun the deer—
I spot a smudge and smokejump in,
spiralling down through my convex lens
that can swell a campfire ring
to a dark lake, then, nearer,
the lost doe's liquid eye
that swallows me in
without a ripple.

WHITE MOONS--

Cynthia Hoffman

Waking

You wake up in the middle of the night knowing
that something has happened to you. The same thing

that has been coming over you slowly
for months the way a patch of weeds

makes its way toward the house. You hang
over the balcony rails and drop the cherry off

the end of your cigarette. Hunched over the rail,
your spine like a boomerang, you remember

every detail like it happened yesterday. The baby-doll
your father took from you and burned. How he

used to hold his arms out and swing himself around
as you and your brother held on

to his biceps, hard as watermelons. How you laughed.
The night he threw your favorite plastic rifle at the wall

for no apparent reason. The morning you found it
up against the sideboard, snapped. Carpet

meeting your bare knees like a bearded kiss.

You turn back into the hall, flush
the cigarette butt down the toilet

press a smooth heel of soap between your palms and the water
slips past like a ponytail. You fall asleep

in an empty house. And sometime while you sleep
your father comes into your room

smacks you over the head
with a rolled-up newspaper

and, saying nothing, turns to go.

You wake up suddenly in the middle of the night
and you know that something has happened to you.

In the weeds along the brick, the beginnings
of a small fire, the fingers of someone buried alive.

Serena Fox

Doc pushes steroids/Family speaks in tongues

and, between the uncharted continents of us, the septic
late amniocentesis ocean of herself, Sillette pulls through.
Mind you,

she has been on "jet fuel" for days—shock lungs, shock liver,
shock kidneys, shock adrenals—fibrin and platelets caulking
and uncaulking

in the everywhere leaking retroperitoneum, uterus a maelstrom
of birth and afterbirth. The infant delivers stillborn, an empty
skiff in

the schooner of her arms, hers and Bill's, before she heads,
hell-bent for the cliffs. We load her with antibiotics, sedatives,
saline,

blood products, catechols. Three young sons enlist us to sign
get-well cards at the nurses' station. Doc pushes steroids.
Family beacons,

coasts, coaxes, keels in tongues. What syllables in its swell?
How the squalling moves and frightens, comforts and sustains
us. It

quiets when we hoist the sign. Another sick ship coming in.
It prays in tidal waves, typhoons, in ripples, ruffles and in
pools. Speaking

tongues. Not stopping, not even when Sillette does. We
dialyse. It is not clear why she does not bleed in rivers to
her death. Then,

six weeks later, she walks out. Wants to try again. Trach is
closing, memory, an undercurrent, not remembering. We are
holds unto

ourselves. There must be body—in and of and around water,
weather, harbor, murmurings not hers or ours—that rocks,
keeps, sings and sails her.

Jeffrey Levine

The Turning

It's not been cold this winter. But tonight—
the ground is hard and grassless, rhododendron leaves
warp tight against the chill,
the sky is clear and piped with stars.

There's the smell of wood smoke and something faintly arctic—
an Inuit's fire—two brown-toothed Eskimos
and their crescent-lidded boys stropping whale bone knives
while drying seal skins by the light.

Later, mom and dad will turn beneath the quilt,
hold quiet while close by their children sleep,
their faces and hands rough, bodies soft as seal skin,
slippery as otters.

Outside, twenty sled dogs huddle, ears cocked
to the faint chop of a single-engine Piper Cub flying
low and toward the moon.

Under the bare cherry trees something still
and ageless seeps up into the bones—
frozen earth, echo of near firesides,
slow breath of the season.

Dora Malech

Statistic

A girl goes missing.

We paint distorted visions
of her body, cling
to the court orders, sleep
with the lights flooding
our eyes.

The pillowcases still smell blue
and clean like her hair,

and bills arrive for the dresses
bought in anticipation of summer.
We pay, watch the flowered fabrics
slump in the closet like empty lungs.

All the faces in the grocery store
are blank and flat as the sides
of milk cartons.

At night, when the windows are open,
she drifts through the screens like heat.

She tiptoes through her mother's
dreams, untangles her hair,
hums softly, tries not to wake her.

Maia McAleavey

Self-Portrait in Duct Tape

This is a list of the things I have built,
things that may not last, that already have not:

balsa-wood car,
papier-mâché volcano,
wax replicas of my hands,
dollhouse, motor, a device
for safe transport of an egg
falling two stories.

Sometimes the durability shocks more than the fall.

The quick ugly fixes: hammering
out the warp, superglue, granny knots,
chopping the loose ends, duct tape.

Even the seamless tongue and groove of rejection and love
is no guarantee of permanence.

Instead, clumsy longevity.
Stickiness.
A holding together.

E. Ethelbert Miller

In A Silent Way

when we were sick
we were very sick of Lincoln Hospital
where one night the doctor told my mother to take
the scarf off her head so he could tie my broken
wrist and I learned that you could not fool my
mother by acting a fool even if you were white and had
one of those things around your neck and someone called

you doctor instead of auntie which is the person I
remember had all the cures for every cousin in Brooklyn

we lived in the Bronx and the stores were
filled with boxes of epsom salt and where
it came from no one would tell and so
we thought it came from the Nile or Mississippi
or from the place where they caught flying fish
and the accents were like bubbles in our ginger ale

one day my grandfather died and my
mother soaked her feet all day long and my father
thought about taking her to the hospital but she
was not sick just humming to herself in a silent way
a sound I would recognize coming from the horn
of Miles years later in an apartment where my lady
scattered my clothes and books across the room
like salt before she left

Larry Moffi

You Cannot Wire Bleeding Hearts

It was his way of killing time, tipping
his watering can to the bleeding hearts
edging his garden each spring just before
Memorial Day, what he still called
Decoration Day for the commendations
and rich colors and dazzle of war's pride,
everything so unlike his quietly bleeding
white and pink hearts.
When Harold died
I was far away from home in Missouri, a town
on the edge of a few broken farms and with
a square around which life's importance
was intended to happen, where pickups
once parked diagonally, motors running
because business would never be better
and to hurry was luxury.

I took my meeting
with a man I'd flown and driven this far
just to listen to, then steered the fuel-
efficient rental car, I think it was a
Stratus or else a Breeze, in a circle
around the square then along an intersect
west. The square diminished, the modest
colors diminished, and the few memorial
crosses and garlands of plastic carnations
propped against them diminished.
The news
had nothing greater to do with itself
but wait in a moderately priced motel
room beside the Interstate. Harold's
wife wanted me for a pallbearer if
there was time. There wasn't. Not
even to return to the square so much in
need of Harold's watering can, his bleeding
hearts, which I learned you cannot wire.

Miriam Mörsel Nathan

Sister Maria Roberta Says the Dead Miss Us and Are Jealous

There's a coffin on the gondola
and the woman going to the funeral
has one hip higher than the other. Her name is
Sister Maria Roberta. Later, over a wooden table,
in the shadow of death and afternoon light,
she fills a white ceramic bowl with pomegranates,
talking of angels. Her favorite is called Pascal.
Sister Maria Roberta talks incessantly and sprinkles aromatic ashes
on bread hot from the oven. *One prayer will take away*
one hour of fire from hell she says. Sister Maria Roberta
grinds seeds, and says *death builds its scratchy nest,*
and carries under his hairy arm the blue straw of our muscles.
Sister Maria Roberta says that five generations of the dead
attend each wedding and even the blind must bless the moon.

Dwaine Rieves

Aubade in E

The wet voice is soft, a slow transfer of touch,
breath returned to the sun, now breast plated and all tense
with spears. So much opening sex, hushed mandates
and decisions—out here the living can't sleep alone.
The proof's one communal array of baby
doves. Yet a voice says questions survive in the unseen,
in a seed's cracked shell, the red core uncontained.
What's left once any lover's gone? It's the soul lifting
both dirty hands, a fall back of flesh to salt,
jeans on the floor, a slow walk home. Today's the first day
of pink lips and unapologetic green,
spring's opera staged within every dying crocus
head. I hear a thousand awkward sounds, the sweet
silence of the body abandoned, a voice the body loved.

Rhonda Williford

The Witness

And this gingko goes all the way back
to first tree—maybe the tree that Adam
lay under, even before the naming,

tossing with some dream—feathery nests,
shining water—traveling toward an image
of Eve which couldn't match the flame-
leaf on fired-maple that she was,

and Eve, unfurling from some unpaired
rib, stirred beneath a mirror-dream—
more smoke and tremor than vision,
and this also not quite Adam, that stretch
of God's imagination, not her own.

And this old ginkgo, from wet-curled roots,
overflows mid-air into a wide lap
for all the coming stories—the blood, iron,
and tinsel—rippling as it catches,
then releases, shimmer and shadow.

And now, Adam, with hand on thigh,
considers, while Eve sighing, leans
breath toward words—their bodies,
not yet touching arch to start all

history—under the ginkgo tree,
casting, in a shake of leaf,
light, dark, light.

Pilar Andrus

Each time I go I am born again,
My mother is bearing me,
Her water breaking,
Fractures in her uteral den.
Every mile from the door is a dilation of her cervix.
The blood is bathing me,
A baptism in the anxiety of my mom,
A shower of screams that people have never heard.
The tears,
Which flow like rivers from the tributaries of mamma's soul,
They merely add to the liquid lubrication of my escape,
The amniotic gasoline that fuels my leave-taking from our home.

And pushing past her embrace
proves harder than caustically forcing my way through the choke-hold of her birth canal,
Carelessly cleaving the fatigued muscles as I continue to move west of my mother's womb.
Contracting,
Compressing,
Tightening the clutch of her vaginal foyer,

A slight corridor to her maternal chamber,
Mamma is advancing my release into the aerated world, which she fears so much,
Breathing,
  Sweating,
    Heaving,
My mother is hurting,
The lines of her creased forehead as numerous as the fearful prayers she says for a safe delivery.

Peter Blair

The Night We Pitch It

Until the TV sails through wet, black air
the bowling balls at the Strand
seem heavy, the linoleum floor in the caged
elevator shaved too thin. Until the TV sails
into the valley of railroad tracks, silent
as a fuse, our flat Iron City drafts
at Lasek's bore into our stomachs and stew.
A steel worker, two roofers, and a printer,
our jobs seem dead ends of our youth
that Sunday night in May when Agnole
says at the light, *I got a busted black and white*
in the trunk to get rid of. The answer
surfaces, inevitable as hills, *Throw it*
off the bridge. Until the TV booms into the empty
coal car, a shower of sparks and glass,
and we hoot and high-five, speeding off the car
like crack high school commandos,
we aren't sure whose side time is on,
playing tackle in the mud, buttoning our nights
with Space Invaders at the Luna,
considering marriage. But there it is, that sound,
filling up the deep beneath us,
and Jim shouting in the car above the rest,
By tomorrow it'll be in Chicago.

WHITE MOONS--

Dan Campbell

Satan's Legions on Weekend Leave

At first all they want is ice water
big gulps, cubes melting in red hot throats.
They drink it standing up, their tails
drooping bull-like behind them, then it's
on to ice cream, eating it with their fingers,
the cream's cream, the party's salvation.

A few even try sex, approaching it
the way you approach a body lying
in the street. But humans are *too* cold.
They'd prefer aliens anytime, devil to alien
humping, the way mutts do it, over and over,
who cares who's watching.
It's a vacation, a chance to lay back,
kick the flame-proof, steel-toed boots off
and watch the soaps.

Believe it or not, devils are shy, especially
about their horns, which so help me Satan,
are sculpted by left-handed blacksmiths.
They spend hours in the tub,
enjoy standing in the rain, and
before reporting back to Hell,
stroll unseen through the mall
and sprinkle phrases into our brain, like

"Hell is filled with the straight and narrow,"
"The serpent is a man's best friend,"

expressions we don't understand at first, but later
we'll suddenly know and laugh the kind of laugh
that scares rats out of their holes
and into the light.

Doug Evans

Sonnet Written in Snow

If I were Inupiaq she'd be snow
falling within the silence of this white

page. My tongue—freezing eight degrees below
my intent. My hand—still trying to write

her. "Impermanence" has become the word
she left written on the moment my eyes

closed like a fist, and I thought I heard
the sound of doors slamming in the reprise

of her fall. I walk in drifts to my throat,
and hang like a noose above my whiskey

'til I can't breathe. In a matchbook, I wrote
our daughter's name and the words "red poppy."

When the snow melts this spring, I will write you.
"...and your eyes—*nascence of the color blue.*"

Patricia Garfinkel

With Mama

I

Then and now,
nothing ever fits
together, knits
together. We were
misfit, from the start.

Born to your trouble,
even tiny I hauled
the brimming pail.

WHITE MOONS--

II

Now you question
everything. You ask,
are you the woman?

Mama, you never
taught me
so I never knew
to wear just one necklace.
I thought impossible
and feminine were
synonyms. I prayed
for sons.

III

On the phone you shout,
is this the medicine?
Remember, Mama, I was
always the medicine.

You are frantic
on a fragile branch.
Again and again, my arms
hurt from the circle
of catching, cradling.

Joanna Howard

The Peacock Reveals Tricks of the Creative Process—And More

He greets me at the stair-top,
a process of feather and grace.

"Watch me," he purrs,
"I'll show you how it's done."
Like a Las Vegas showgirl,
he balances each step,
weighs his burden,
reaches the landing, and

turning, deals a fan of feathers,
shuffling shag, revealing blues,
blending emeralds,
an audience of eyes. . .

From where I stand,
all I've seen is his backside:
how it's done by this
plump, rumple of a bird,
with white black underwings,
which he scratches on days off,
while practicing, mending, mulling
feather stretching, perfecting.

Again he pivots, eyeing me—
I know. I've seen how he does it,
this brilliant cakewalk of life,
what it takes to balance wing and feather,
to preen and repair, to sweat magic.

Bert Hubinger

Nancy Reagan Looks to the East and Turns to Salt

Even as she waves,
she whitens, crystalline
the fingers, block-like
stumps the legs.
Nancy now becomes
her porcelain,
looking back toward
Kremlin walls.
Advisers warned, don't
look back,
ratings will crumble,
dynasties fall. Yeats
revives and moans,
Our God is dust, our
God is prisoner of

WHITE MOONS-

special interest. But
once in a while we hear
from the past. Don't
look back. You will
surely turn to salt,
and cows will lick
your monument.
The face is blurred,
melting, returning to
the sea. You will never
wonder how it happened,
never see or hear
the lone humpback
or great white sperm
beating up against the bland
actors, laughing at their
loose portrayals, their
unconvincing roles.
The whale cruises
up the delta searching for
the source. The source is
ours. Even a parasite
knows how to find it,
up the river,
beyond the salt.

Lisa Kosow

Aubade

Morning splits open, drops pearls into out-
stretched hands. I step into glass-splintered light
that spills across the floor. Clock hands point south
to blue that paints over hours of night.

Eggs crack in a skillet skimmed with butter,
low flame firms them into yellow-eyed globes.

Slick taste of eggs, creatures unborn stutter
in my mouth, light leaks pale from the window.

Water rings as I turn the faucet, think
of chanterelles, salmon runs, rivers slow,
winding while my hours wait on rails, in
cities of pigeon clouds and money flow.

The day spins out, I step out to its beat,
white shells and sidewalks crack beneath my feet.

Katherine Plimpton

...a conversation...

i've held my tongue
and allowed you to mispronounce
the understanding of myself

and i wonder if this is what you meant
when you said that we needed to

"relearn the patterns of silence"

you must have caught me in one of those moments
when we hold hour glasses to our souls

and i forgot to count the seconds
between the different faces of death

because you've painted hands
on the bellies of my bruises
and told me now i have somewhere to lay the blame

WHITE MOONS--

Jonathan Vaile

Climate

Knowing the terrier is terrified
of thunder, we return from the reading
in time to console him before
the fronts collide, before the falling
of the sky—

and even as my toes test
the temperature in the tub, you're holding
him still, on the floor in the hallway, telling him
how poetry moved you tonight—

and so, when the weatherman
from somewhere in the living room
says *let's put the clouds in motion,* you implore me
to turn it all off just for once, to open

the window and light only candles,
to return to the tub
with any anthology and read aloud
to no one
but the two of you.

Reed Whittemore

The Schools

the schools will not let you go
but sit on their hills with their chapels and dining halls
and when you have moved out and down to the world
they send you letters about the chapels and dining halls

and what a good time you had in the chapels and dining halls
back in the Iron Age when you took German
and Herr von Schmalz
put his paunch in the middle drawer at nine every morning

yes

the letters with pictures of chapels and dining halls
keep being mailed down down to the world
with news of President Whosis and Herr von Schmalz
and the costs of the new ski tow

even when you say no no more letters no
for the schools on the hills will not let you go
                                        ever go

Jennifer Atkinson

Three Years: a Composition in Gesso and Graphite

From the drowned marsh-island lumbers the osprey.

Low inland fog annuls the creek and byways, all
But the tallest, tasseled reeds. Like sleep

Mist overtakes rank distance and detail,
Near and far, the expanse of wind-

Trampled salt hay, the stiff seedcrowns
At the creek edge. What dream is this

That your refusal should lie so quiet,
Your heart the palm-up concave of a clamshell?

What cold dream that only the osprey, hunting, wakes?

WHITE MOONS-

Ned Balbo

Red Planet

Overnight Mars will become the playground of the solar system...
—*LIFE,* May '91

Our choices are endless. Take, for instance,
Mars—
Long burned-out
beach without an ocean where
light gravity invites tall leaps
past canyons, over cliffs—*And that's just*
fine, you think as you soar toward
the midpoint of your arc and peer out
from your pressure-suit as you imagine
owning a world bereft
of waterfalls and rivers, a world where
red dust glitters down
from glazed plateaus...

Yes, it's beautiful, you think—
The station's slanting into sight; you know now
that you'll soon be home, you'll let
your loved one knead your shoulders
while the lava geysers rise in white-gold
bursts on the horizon, vast drills
tearing through the dried crust, spiralling
downward to the core—*Yes, we could*
surely have it all—you steady your boots
on your descent, knowing well
when nightfall comes, you'll land
and hurry back to base before
the temperature-fall freeze-dries you—
pink dust swirls up toward the stars—
And in
the shadow of boiling vats, you touch down
on the pitted landscape, quarry scars
and tire tracks, glancing once more

at the horizon—*There,*
where once a blue gem floated,
and our need was merciless—*Yes, there—*

where one red speck still cuts
across the sky.

Anne Marie Blum

Scars

We map our lives by them,
connect the dots of what we've endured,
provoked, so that we never entirely forget
the moment the scissors slipped
by accident, by will,
or when the coffee was hurled
faster than epithets.

We think we've buried the drama
in the mind's backyard
or pruned it to the root,
until we glance down
and see scars flowering the body—
a garden of milkweed
and pale, pale rosettes.

Barbara DeCesare

Native

There are no Mafia stories at the table.
Mostly we are cowards in my family,
unable to fully invest
in the worst we have to offer.

WHITE MOONS-

My father's mother loved a man
who murdered a family friend,
but she married the one with clear eyes,
came over on a boat and changed my name
to pronounceable syllables,
native sounds.
She kept the sheets clean,
the closets closed.

The adults only swear in Italian.

My brown skin glows in the summer sun,
my English is perfect
my blood has been transfused. It's better.
I am better. Singular and lean,
falling asleep in my rocking boat.
I don't remember launching from shore.

Ruth Dickey

"Puellas" (girls), 1992

Magdalena Abakanowicz, Polish Sculptor
Smithsonian Sculpture Garden

30 figures stand at attention in the trees
arms at their sides
headless
cast bronze giving them sinewy bodies
their veins more prominent than skin

2 are turned away, keeping watch
the rest face the fountain and the tourists
they are the bodies of headless 11 year olds
with differing shapes before puberty's wand touches them
the realization they are girls creeps up on me
and taps me on the shoulder

just then
the tourist in the bright madras shorts

and white sandals
readjusts her sunglasses
looks at them, shakes her head
"poor things" she tells her son

but they do not strike me as poor things
standing at attention
there in the trees
30, a class size
perhaps lined up before puberty
to carefully learn the lesson that girls' bodies
are more important than their heads
30, perhaps the artist's age
each year of her youth a soldier
headless for things forgotten
30, perhaps 30 warnings
30 pounds a woman wants to lose
30 days in a menstrual cycle
30 catcalls in the street
30 "no"s
30 things left undone

Neal Dwyer

Insomnia Notebook

More and more of her is always awake
there's so much less of her to know.

She dreams with her eyes open
of a life that tastes like lemonade—but settles,
as she will, for a job at an all-night gas station
and smokes unfiltered cigarettes
and does her nails.

She sees herself as an infomercial; the passing
interest of channel surfers lands on her price: cheap,
and her *Life-Back-If-Not-Completely-Satisfied*
return policy.

But she breaks as often around three a.m.
when there is no traffic, and she dives into the dark
above a streetlight. And there is no word
for that.

Maybe one day she'll sleep a long way.
Maybe one day she'll feel blood coursing through
her like a warm current, not like a storm drain
flowing with bits of broken glass.

Maybe one day she'll emerge victorious;
a tatoo on her thigh, a navel ring, and a day job.

Erich Hintze

Instructions

When you're this old,
you care less about their eyes,
their hair, their height
but their wrists and stomachs
still need thin flatness
like wafers or knives; this way,
you'll know better whether or not
she'll be missed and by whom:
their names and faces clear
and easy for her will come
from her mouth or womb for you
all for you
every pound of her.

It's like Brenda in Atlanta
vodka tonic and twist.
Or Rachel in Charlotte
where all the children are beautiful
and *what were the names of hers?*

To start, you won't need anything above
what's available at Hechinger's

so watch the weekend specials
and buy everything on sale.

You know they've slept with men
they didn't know well
or thought they knew better
so just smile, lean forward,
tell her she's beautiful.
When she says "No"
say *yes*!

Sally Rosen Kindred

Earth Science

for Jenny Berggren

I loved the Doppler effect for Sam,
the black Lab whose head shone
from the window of the red Ford

as Mr. Fenske drove past his pack
of students immersed in sun.
He drove by with his hand on the horn,

which is where Doppler came in, but better
was the black flap-eared bliss at the window
out of March, better the tongue's swagger

in the cracked-open air. We were thirteen,
viscous and secreting new warmth,
and this was why we were in love

with the earth, with its tender mass of
panting gratitude, its cool nails
ticking on the tiles under the padded weight

of an old dog's body, its hope as we'd stood up
before the tables black
with the study of grime

WHITE MOONS--

and watched the teacher open the dark door into spring.
This was three years before Challenger,
before Sam's best friend gained fame

as the teacher who did not die in space.
It was early in the evolution of our flesh
and damp in that small room. But now we were released

and Sam's tongue hung thick and pink, telling us
who we were: not Doppler, who thought he knew
how sound gave and withdrew; not sound

which wove between our bones in daring chords.
We were the dog, our heads poured
from the vinyl heart of the dark car, our eyes sopped

in sun, tongues dipped in motion's sweat.
This was the reason we studied the earth, to learn
why air after rain smells like concrete and skin,

to talk about earth so it filled our wet mouths,
to let it heat our fine black fur
as we hurtled into April, space and time and sun.

Shan Shi

Forgetfulness is an act. Of enormous will.
It is not for the nostalgic or weak-hearted.
Life is not a vehicle prone to forgetfulness.
It will drive you right up to the curb of Memory
and wake you screaming in the night, begging
for a little forgetfulness.
Begging for a little relief.

Greg McBride

Spooning

A spoon
lies sturdy
in repose,
its arc of
neck like
yours, and
yields to
my light
touch—
a finger
slide
along
the
nape
down
down
to
ample
bowl.
See how
yours and mine,
on edge, married tip
to heel, lie as if designed
to meet in this satin box
in such economy of
space, and so met,
to sleep.

Sarah Stillman

A Bun in Barbie's Oven

It strikes me as strange,
this Pregnant Barbie in Aisle Four,
a ripe melon protruding
from her tight plastic flesh.

WHITE MOONS--

What is waiting in there
to be born?

I try to picture Barbie
lying, sweaty, next to Ken
in their pink Victorian bed.
But her legs won't spread
more than a centimeter
and her arms can't wrap
around his rippled chest.

I envision Barbie's face
as she lies flat upon the delivery table,
paralyzed with fear, unable to scream,
lips frozen in that blind, joyous smile.

J. D. Smith

Aubade

Dog, and I believe that I can call you that
with a high degree of accuracy,
in a purely denotative sense, though,
unsullied by cultural associations,
please listen,
since I seldom ask that much of you
(the couch is yours no less than mine,
the pillows, past and present, more so):
You would, if you a possessed a consciousness
of cause and effect, self and other
and the mortality that swallows them,
be grateful to know nothing
beyond that which you know right now
because, for me,
it's seven-thirty on a partly cloudy
Tuesday, forty-five degrees,
with a sixty-percent chance of rain
and the certainty
of a commute and a day's work

in which I'll be wagged by—appended to—
devices engineered by men
who get out even less than me.
Really, they exist,
though you might have gathered otherwise
from the long and many evenings that we share—
like tonight, when we'll
resume this small symposium.
Until then, fellow traveler on the planet,
don't scratch that spot behind your ear—
it's already bare.
A new rawhide bone is on your bed
and, as always, *cane mio,*
the kibble's in the bowl.

Thom Stuart

Death was

by the screened porch, where the downspout sipped
the runnel's indigo back, wet with moon,
    and the shrubs and flower-beds reveled in neglect.

in the kitchen, roused with cottons on balmy
tussles, or leaning on a game board aslant
    under the breakfront.

in the bedroom, where the garments lay
throttled for the boxes or the freakish midway's plastic,
    while a useless pair of glasses on the nightstand looked away.

on the dresser, in a bracelet tree, holding down the colors—
no matter that we moved or breathed, the air drooped
    in flecky scrims and worn-out breaths, colorless.

in the living room, unhid, confessed
with muss along the tatty roughs
    of pasts bare on the pile.

WHITE MOONS--

in the corner, bunched with homeless lamps, plotting
shapes at blatant walls— a stenciled brattice shored
against the caving in.

in silence and words almost said— jags that bury slowly,
like stones in sucking mud— still, my confabulating eyes denied
that place had lost its sense of place.

in a scent, not easy for a house or room,
in the angle of a lone chair—
death was in every little thing, everywhere.

Charlotte Gould Warren

Sons

Gone! As if they'd
never been. The great madrona
quiet in a quiet rain,
cut wood greyed from years
left out in the weather,
patchy winter grass.
Not even deer prints.

I watch my breath condense
on the window in a milky
sparkle. Three swans
fly overhead, close and white,
their stretched-out necks
and fabulous wings, gabbling and singing
in a language the body instantly registers.

Even after they disappear,
the blaze of their wingbeats
keeps on arriving, their voices
overtaking me,
imprinted like loss,
like discovery:
breath, blood, bone.

The Word Works Young Poets Competition Winners

In 1988, Karren Alenier designed the Young Poets Competition and had Gail Ranadive develop and run the first competition as part of her M.F.A. graduate studies at The American University. Over the years, the program has been organized and carried out by such poets and teachers as Maxine Clair, Lisa Horwitz, Elaine Magarrell, Mary Quattlebaum, Betty Stegall, Jodi Suleiman, and, currently, Perry Epes.

Each year, the winners, selected from among some 20 participating area high-schools, read at the Miller Cabin with an award-winning poet.

1988	Laura Flippin and Robin Suleiman reading with Roland Flint
1989	Tamara Gawthrop and Deborah Wassertzug reading with Susan Sonde
1990	Melissa Levine and Sarah DeWeerdt reading with Lucille Clifton
1991	Tracee Rhodes and Sonja Weisel reading with Richard Harteis
1992	Guang-Shing Cheng and Cristina Brown reading with Faye Moskowitz
1993	Erica Weitzman and Jennifer Dante reading with Stanley Plumly
1994	Ann Strom and Kim Linn reading with Michael Collier
1995	Lisa Cantey and Craig McEldowney reading with Merrill Leffler
1996	Joe Bawol and Elizabeth Hazen reading with Rod Jellema
1997	Jennifer LeRoy and Melissa Marshall reading with John Callahan
1998	Michelle Gil-Montero and Damon Talbott reading with Anne Caston
1999	Dora Malech and Maia McAleavey reading with E. Ethelbert Miller
2000	Pilar Andrus and Katherine Plimpton reading with Reed Whittemore
2001	Shan Shi and Sarah Stillman reading with Jennifer Atkinson

National Public Television films Miller Cabin reading by Lucille Clifton and Young Poets Melissa Levine and Sandra DeWeert, 1990. STANDING: *Near tree, Michael Albo and Joe Ross;* SEATED: *Buck Downs, Lucky Wentworth;* LYING DOWN: *Jimmy Banks.*

Top:
Seated, Jacklyn Potter, Marjory Innes, David Barrows, Betsy Wollaston and Michael Davis are loyal members of the audience.

Center:
Chris Bursk, Susan Mercury, Robert Sargent, Howard Gofreed and Mary Ann Daly focus on the poet and the poem.

Bottom:
Katherine Harnett Shaw, Susan Sonde and Barbara Goldberg enjoy a Kennedy Street reception.

CABIN FEVER--

About the Poets

Ally Acker is the author of two collections of poems, *Surviving Desire* (1994), winner of the Garden Street Press Award, and *Waiting for the Beloved* (The Valentine Publishing Group, 1999). She resides in New York and conducts movement and writing workshops.

Jane Alberdeston, a performing poet, was co-founder of the Modern Urban Griots, and a fellow of Cave Canem. In 2001, she received a D.C. Commission on the Arts and Humanities grant. Jane has produced two books of poetry, *The Waters of My Thirst* and *The AfroTaina Dreams.*

Karren Alenier has authored five collections of poetry, including *Looking for Divine Transportation* (The Bunny & the Crocodile Press). Winner of the 2002 Towson University Prize for Literature, she co-edited *Winners: A Retrospective of the Washington Prize* (The Word Works, 1999). Her work has appeared in *Mississippi Review, Negative Capability, Poet Lore* and she is currently working on an opera about Gertrude Stein.

Elizabeth Alexander's collections of poetry include *Antebellum Dream Book* (Graywolf Press, 2001), *Body of Life* (1996) and *The Venus Hottentot* (1990).

Fareedah Allah has been published in the following anthologies: *New Poets Generation* (California); *WPFW 89.5 FM Poetry Anthology* (Bunny & Crocodile Press), *Say That the River Turns* (Chicago), and *Letters to America* (Detroit). She holds an M.Ed. from Howard and teaches in Washington, D.C.

Nathalie Anderson's book, *Following Fred Astaire* (The Word Works, 1998), won the Washington Prize. She directs the Program in Creative Writing and is a Professor of English Literature at Swarthmore College. A 1993 Pew Fellow in the Arts, she is also a librettist whose operas have been produced by the Philadelphia Orchestra, 2001.

Pilar Andrus was a co-winner for the 2000 Young Poets Competition.

Barri Armitage's book, *Double Helix,* won publication by the Washington Writers' Publishing House in 1992. Her poems have appeared in *Poetry, The Georgia Review, Poet Lore*, and two editions of *Anthology of Magazine Verse & Yearbook of American Poetry.*

Renée Ashley's poetry collections include *Salt* (Wisconsin, Brittingham Prize, 1991), *The Various Reasons of Light* (Avocet, 1998), and *The Revisionist's Dream* (Avocet, 2001). She received an NEA Fellowship for 1997-1998 and her work is included in the Pushcart Prize XXIV (2000).

Jennifer Atkinson is the author of two collections of poetry, *The Dogwood Tree* (University of Alabama) and *The Drowned City* (Northeastern University Press) which won the 2000 Samuel French Morse Prize. She lives in Fairfax, Virginia, and teaches poetry writing at George Mason University.

Mark Baechtel is a lecturer in English at Grinnell College, Iowa, and has published poetry in *American Literary, Lip Service* and *Poet Lore.* His fiction has appeared in *Sou'wester*, and he has written book reviews and features for *The Washington Post.* He holds an M.F.A. from the Iowa Writers' Workshop.

Ned Balbo's collection, *Galileo's Banquet* (Washington Writers' Publishing House, 1998), won the Towson University Prize. Three times a Pushcart Prize nominee and twice a Fellow at the Virginia Center for Creative Arts, his poems have appeared in *Antioch Review, APR, Crab Orchard Review,* and the *Notre Dame Review.*

HOLLY BASS has poems appearing or forthcoming in *Callaloo*, the *Washington Review,* and the anthology, *Role Call* (Third World Press, 2001). She is also a dancer and performance artist who has presented work at the Kennedy Center, Arena Stage, Whitney Museum and St. Mark's Poetry Project.

ANNE BECKER's book, *The Transmutation Notebooks: Poems in the Voices of Charles and Emma Darwin,* appeared in 1996. Recently a selection, in translation, was included in *Calicanto*, a literary journal from Manzanares, Spain. She conducts a poetry workshop for those affected by their own or a family member's life-threatening illness.

MEL BELIN's first book of poetry, *Flesh That Was Chrysalis,* was published by The Word Works in 1999. He is a graduate of Dartmouth College, and George Washington University Law School, and currently resides in Arlington, Virginia.

PATRICIA BERTHEAUD received her M.F.A. from George Mason University. Her poetry has appeared in *The American Poetry Review* and *Phoebe*. She has also taught poetry writing at Montgomery County Community College in Pennsylvania. She is currently a home health nurse living in Pennsylvania with her husband and two sons.

DAVID BIESPIEL's recent collection of poems is *Shattering Air* (BOA Editions). Recipient of an NEA Fellowship and the Wallace Stegner Fellowship, he is poet-in-residence at The Attic, in Portland, Oregon.

PETER BLAIR's most recent collection of poems, *Last Heat* (The Word Works, 1999), won the Washington Prize. His work has appeared in *Crazyhorse, Poetry East,* and *West Branch,* and he has received two Pennsylvania Council On the Arts fellowships for poetry.

ANGIE BLAKE-MOORE has published her work in *Dodobobo, The Mojo Sloth, The Potomac Review,* and *The Peralta Press.* She teaches 3 and 4-year-olds in Washington, D.C., and lives in Alexandria with her husband and baby girl.

DEAN BLEHERT's latest books are *Please Lord, Make Me a Famous Poet or at Least Less Fat,* and a new chapbook, *Kill the Children,* from The Argonne House Press.

ANNE MARIE BLUM's poems have appeared in *Rattapallax, Visions International,* and *Green Mountain Review.* She received the 1985 Brother Leonard Mann Poetry Award from the University of Dayton, and her play, "Café de L'Espoir," was produced by the New Works Theater in 1994. She lives in Reston, Virginia.

JOHN BRADLEY is the editor of *Atomic Ghost: Poets Respond to the Nuclear Age* and *Learning to Glow: A Nuclear Reader*. His book, *Love-In-Idleness: The Poetry of Roberto Zingarello* (The Word Works), won the 1989 Washington Prize. He teaches writing at Northern Illinois University.

DORIS BRODY is a Jenny McKean Moore fellow in creative writing (George Washington University) and has published and read her work widely. She holds degrees from Michigan State and the University of Wisconsin and toiled as a science writer for 20 years.

CHRISTOPHER BURSK is the author of seven books, including *The Way Water Rubs Stone* (The Word Works) and, most recently, *Ovid at Fifteen*, from New Issues Press.

DAN CAMPBELL was interviewed for the "Poet to Poet" television show in New York City and has published his poems in *Rattapallax* and *Medicinal Purposes*. One of his poems was made into a song for a chamber opera at the Hirschorn Museum in Washington, D.C.

RICK CANNON has taught secondary and college English for the past twenty-six years, and he currently co-edits *Poet Lore*. His work is featured in numerous publications, and he has won two Maryland Arts Council Grants in poetry.

NANCY NAOMI CARLSON's work has appeared in *Poetry, Shenandoah, Prairie Schooner, Poet Lore* and *Cimarron Review,* and was featured on "Poetry Daily." *Kings Highway* was published by the Washington Writers' Publishing House in 1997. She is an editor for Tupelo Press and conducts a writer's group for Barnes & Noble.

KENNETH CARROLL, who teaches literature at Duke Ellington High School, has poems in *Black Literature Forum, Catalyst Magazine, African Commentary, NOMMO, Konch Magazine* and the anthology, *Hungry As We Are* (Washington Writers' Publishing House, 1995). His poetry collection is *So What: For The White Dude Who Said This Ain't Poetry* (Bunny & Crocodile Press, 1997).

ANNE CASTON's first collection of poems, *Flying Out with the Wounded,* won the 1996 New York University Press Prize for Poetry. Her poems have been anthologized in such collections as *Where Books Fall Open* and in *The New American Poets: A Bread Loaf Anthology.* She is currently working on a second collection of poems.

GRACE CAVALIERI is the author of eleven books of poetry and numerous plays. The latest, *Pinecrest Rest Haven,* was based on The Word Works book of the same title and was produced in New York City in 2001. Grace produces and hosts "The Poet and the Poem" from the Library of Congress for Public Radio.

LUCILLE CLIFTON's book, *Blessing the Boats: New and Selected Poems 1988-2000* (BOA Editions, 2000), won the National Book Award in 2001. She has published numerous other award-winning books. She is a Chancellor of The Academy of American Poets and a Distinguished Professor of Humanities at St. Mary's College of Maryland.

SHIRLEY C. COCHRANE, who also writes fiction, has recently published *Letters to the Quick/Letters to the Dead* (1998), blending parts of two earlier poetry collections with new work. She has also published *The Fair-haired Boy* (The Word Works, 1997), a fiction chapbook.

DON COLBURN is a reporter for *The Oregonian* in Portland. Before that he was a reporter for 16 years at *The Washington Post.* He holds an M.F.A. from Warren Wilson College and his poems have appeared in *The Iowa Review, The Nation, Prairie Schooner* and *Virginia Quarterly Review.* He has been a finalist for the Pulitzer Prize in feature writing.

MICHAEL COLLIER is the author of four books of poems including *The Ledge,* a finalist for the National Book Critics Circle Award, 2000. He is co-director of Creative Writing at the University of Maryland, College Park, and currently serves as the Poet Laureate of the State of Maryland.

ANDREA COLLINS is a writer living in Washington D.C. She is a Katy Lehman Fellow and M.F.A. graduate of the Writing Program at Pennsylvania State University. Her work has appeared in *Agni, College English, Southern Review* and other periodicals. Her literary volunteer gigs include the Literary Café at Art-o-Matic, and a year of hosting Cafe Musé at Strathmore Hall.

GAIL COLLINS-RANADIVE is a Unitarian Universalist minister serving congregations in transition; thus she moves every year. Her book of writing exercises for women, first published in 1992, was recently reissued under a new title, *Finding the Voice Inside: Writing as a Spiritual Quest for Women* (Skinner House).

SARAH COTTERILL's poems have appeared widely in journals, including *American Poetry Review, Poetry Northwest,* and *Ploughshares*. Her collection, *In the Nocturnal Animal House,* was published in 1991 by Purdue University Press.

MARK CRAVER, who teaches high school and at George Mason University, has published: *The Problem of Grace* (1986), *Seven Crowns for the White Lady of the Other World* and *Blood Poems* (1992), *They Come for What You Love* (1998), and *Team First, Team Last: An Epic Journey to the Heart of High School Basketball* (2000).

LOIS CUCULLU is an assistant professor of English at the University of Minnesota where she teaches literature. She is completing a book on modernism and the cult of the expert entitled, *The Female Intellectual and Modernist Clerisy.* Her work has appeared in such journals as *differences, Novel, A Forum on Fiction, TSLL,* and *Colorado Review.*

MARY ANN DALY runs the phone system at a Washington think tank. Her poems have appeared in *Poet Lore, Lip Service, Carolina Quarterly,* various anthologies, and most recently in *The New Millennium Harp,* a collection of hymns in the Sacred Harp tradition.

ENID DAME's books of poems include *Anything You Don't See* (West End, 1992), *On the Road to Damascus, Maryland* (Downtown Poets, 1980) and *Stone Sheknina* (Three Mile Harbor, 2003). She was co-winner of the Many Mountains Moving literary award in 1997.

HEATHER DAVIS received an M.A. in Creative Writing from Syracuse University in 1992. She has published poems in *Poet Lore, Puerto del Sol, Sonora Review, Cream City Review, Slipstream, Route One,* and other journals. She lives in Alexandria, Virginia.

JOSEPH DAVIS has published poems in *WordWrights!, Potpourri,* and *Dream International Quarterly.* He is an environmental journalist widely published in his field and holds a Ph.D. in English and American Language and Literature from the University of Michigan.

MICHAEL C. DAVIS lives and plays guitar in Arlington, Virginia. His poetry has appeared in *Poet Lore, Lip Service*, and *Minimus* and the anthologies *Open Door* and *Winners: A Retrospective of the Washington Prize* (The Word Works, 1999). He published a chapbook, *Upon Waking,* in 1997. He is a poet and artist in the schools.

PATRICIA DAVIS earned an M.F.A. from American University, where she was poetry editor of *Folio* magazine and received two Lannan fellowships. She has poems published or forthcoming in *Salt Hill Review, Potomac Review,* and *Puerto del Sol.* A nonfiction book, *The Blindfold's Eyes,* which she co-authored with her sister, Diana Ortiz, was published in 2002 by Orbis Books.

BARBARA DECESARE's first book, *jigsaweyesore*, was called "What thunder looks like in writing," by *The Baltimore Sun.* She received an M.F.A. from Goddard College and resides with her three children in York, Pennsylvania.

JOANNE "ROCKY" DELAPLAINE, a social justice activist, has published in *Other Testaments, Volume I, The Old Testament.* She's conducted poetry workshops at the Great Labor Arts Exchange and has read at many venues.

RUTH DICKEY, founder of Miriam's Kitchen forum for homeless writers, is also co-founder of mothertongue, D.C. women's spoken word. She has taught poetry and creative writing in homeless shelters, soup kitchens and public schools, and has been honored by the Larry Neal Writing Award.

MOSHE DOR, born in Tel Aviv, is the author of some 35 books in Hebrew. His most recent book in English translation is *Khamsin: Memoirs and Poetry by a Native Israeli.* His work has been translated into some twenty languages. His honors include the Prime Minister's Prize and the Bialik Prize, Israel's top literary award.

BUCK DOWNS lives and works in Washington, D.C. His book, *marijuana soft drink,* was published by Edge Books in 2000.

NEAL DWYER's poetry has appeared in *The Iowa Review, Tar River Poetry,* and other journals in the U.S. and France. He has studied poetry at the University of Nice, France, and at George Mason University. He teaches English and French at the College of Southern Maryland, where he also edits the literary magazine, *Connections.*

SEAN ENRIGHT's poems and reviews have appeared in *Threepenny Review, The Kenyon Review, The Sewanee Review, The American Scholar* and *Tikkun*, among others. He is also author of a novel, *Goof and Other Stories*, and teaches poetry workshops at the Writer's Center in Bethesda, Maryland. Sean is married and has two children.

W. PERRY EPES is Chair of the English Department at Episcopal High School in Alexandria, Virginia. He holds an M.F.A. in Poetry from George Mason University and has published poems in *Phoebe, Negative Capability,* and *GW Forum.* He coordinates the annual Young Poets Competition for The Word Works.

CABIN FEVER--

Doug Evans has spent a year and a half finishing his first chapbook, *Promising Salvation to Strays.* His poems have appeared in *Frantic Egg,* and he founded the Revolution Poetry Series in Herndon, Virginia.

Roland Flint, the late Poet Laureate of Maryland, enjoyed a national reputation. He wrote seven books of poems including *Easy, Stubborn, Resuming Green,* and *Say It.* He taught at Georgetown University and helped launch many young writers from his classes and workshops.

Linda Nemec Foster is the author of six books of poetry. The most recent, *Amber Necklace from Gdansk* (Louisiana State University, 2001) has been nominated for several awards including the Laughlin Award from the Academy of American Poets. Her poems have appeared in *The Georgia Review, Nimrod, DoubleTake,* and *Sou'wester*.

Serena J. Fox is a local physician who has been published in *The Paris Review, JAMA, Squaw Valley Review*. She holds a B.A. with a tripartite major in Biology, History, and Arts and Letters.

Lillian Frankel has published 17 books in the juvenile field, edited children's magazines, and written humorous essays for *The Washington Post.* She recently won a Maryland State Arts Council grant to write poems about the Great Depression and read them in senior citizen facilities.

Sunil Freeman is the Assistant Director of the Writer's Center. He has published a book of poems, *That Would Explain the Violinist* (Gut Punch Press, 1993), and a chapbook, *Surreal Freedom Blues* (Argonne House Press, 1999). His poems have appeared in journals and anthologies, and he has received a Maryland State Arts Council grant.

Karlis Freivalds was born in Brooklyn, New York, two years after his family moved from Latvia. His books include *Sylvia, A Riga Nocturne* (Black Buzzard Press).

Nan Fry is the author of two collections of poetry: *Relearning the Dark* (Washington Writers'Publishing House) and *Say What I Am Called* (Sibyl-Child). One of her poems appears in the anthology *Poetry in Motion: From Coast to Coast* (W.W. Norton).

Martin Galvin has published over 300 poems. *Wild Card* (Washington Writers' Publishing House, 1989) won the Columbia Book Award, judged by Howard Nemerov. Other prizes include the Narrative Poetry Award (1992) from *Poet Lore* and first prize in the 1999 *Potomac Review* poetry competition. His work appeared in *The Best American Poetry 1997.*

Patricia Garfinkel has published three books of poetry. The latest is *Making The Skeleton Dance* (George Braziller, 2000). Many of her poems have appeared in journals and anthologies, and she has taught speech writing and poetry workshops.

Tamara Gawthrop works in the printing industry and resides quietly in the Virginia countryside with two cats and hundreds of books.

David Gewanter is the author of *In the Belly* (U. Chicago, 1997), and co-editor of the *Collected Poems of Robert Lowell* (FSG, 2003). He won the John C. Zacharis First Book Award, the Witter Bynner Fellowship and a Whiting Award. He teaches at Georgetown University and is completing a new book of poems entitled *Sleep of Reason*.

Michelle Gil-Montero is a senior at Brown University where she is working on her honors manuscript in poetry with poet Forrest Gander. Her work has been published in Brown publications *Somos* and *The Indy*, and she serves as the managing editor of *Glimpse Magazine.*

Brian Gilmore is a lawyer and author of two collections of poetry: *elvis presley is alive and well and living in harlem* (Third World Press, 1993) and *Jungle Nights and Soda Fountain Rags: Poem for Duke Ellington* (Karibu Books, 2000).

Howard Gofreed's poems recently appeared in *WordWrights*!

Bina Goldfield lives in New York City. Her chapbook is *Blade Against the Skin* (Singular Speech Press, 1991), and her poems have appeared in numerous anthologies and literary magazines.

PAUL GRANT, a native of Louisiana, has had poems in *Georgia Review, Sewanee Review, Crazyhorse* and other magazines. He lives in western Maryland and is poetry editor of *Antietam Review*.

PATRICIA GRAY received a 2002 Artist Fellowship for poetry from the D.C. Commission on the Arts and Humanities. Her poems have appeared in *WordWrights!, forpoetry.com, Cider Press Review, Poetry International, Shenandoah* and *The MacGuffin*.

HERBERT S. GUGGENHEIM is a social worker in Washington, D.C., and an adjunct English Professor at the University of the District of Columbia. He studied writing at Johns Hopkins University and has published poems in the *Beloit Poetry Journal, New Collage,* and the *Washington Review*. His chapbook *Pomes, Buck Each* appeared in 1994.

DANIEL GUTSTEIN's work has appeared or is forthcoming in *Ploughshares, Prairie Schooner, TriQuarterly, The American Scholar, Fiction, Story Quarterly,* and elsewhere. A former economist and farmhand, editor and tae kwon do instructor, he currently teaches creative writing to students with disabilities at George Washington University.

PAUL HAENEL, a native of Pittsburgh, has lived for 20 years in the D.C. area where he has published his first collection of poems, *Farewell, Goodbye, Wave Goodbye* (Washington Writers' Publishing House, 1994). His work has appeared most recently in *Potomac Review*.

CATHRYN HANKLA is the author of nine books of poetry and fiction, the latest of which are *Poems for the Pardoned* (Louisiana State University, 2002) and the novel, *The Land Between* (Baskerville, 2003).

MARGARET HANZIMANOLIS, a teacher in Vermont and Ph.D. candidate in colonial-era South African literature at the University of Cape Town, South Africa, has translations of Argentinian Alfonsina Storni in a number of journals. Her poems have appeared in *Feminist Review, Beloit Poetry Journal, Virginia Review* and the *Mid-American Review*.

LINDA LEE HARPER's six collections of poetry include *Toward Desire* (The Word Works, 1996) and *Blue Flute* (Adastra Press, 1999). She works in the English Department, University of South Carolina-Aiken and lives in Augusta, Georgia.

JEFFREY HARRISON is the author of three poetry collections, *The Singing Underneath* (a National Poetry Series selection, 1988), *Signs of Arrival* (1996), and *Feeding The Fire* (Sarabande, 2001). He was a Guggenheim Fellow in 1999 and recently taught at Phillips Academy for three years as the Roger Murray Writer-in-Residence.

RICHARD HARTEIS is the author of ten books of poetry and fiction, most recently the novel, *Sapphire Dawn* (Vivisphere Books), and *Provence, New and Selected Poems* (Vivisphere Books). He lives in Uncasville, Connecticut, and West Palm Beach, Florida.

LOLA HASKINS' newest collection of poems is *The Rim Benders* (Anhinga, 2001). Her work has appeared in *The Atlantic Monthly, The Christian Science Monitor, The London Review of Books, Georgia Review, Southern Review* and *Prairie Schooner*. She won the Iowa Poetry Prize for *Hunger* (Iowa, 1993) and the Emily Dickinson/*Writer Magazine* Award.

WENDELL HAWKEN has published a chapbook, *Mother Tongue* (Argonne House Press, 2001), and her poems have appeared in *Poet Lore, The Roanoke Review, Bogg, Starfish Haiku, Calyx, Snowy Egret, Comstock Review,* and others. She still tends her cows and horses.

AVA LEAVELL HAYMON's newest book *The Strict Economy of Fire* is forthcoming from Louisiana State University Press. She is also a playwright and directs the Guadalupe Mesa Writers and Artists Studio in New Mexico each summer. She once met the grand-nephew of Joaquin Miller in Monterrey, Mexico.

ROBERT HAYNES lives in Scottsdale, Arizona. He is the author of *The Grand Unified Theory* (Kansas City, Paladin Contemporaries, 2001), a book-length poem. His

CABIN FEVER--

poems have appeared in *New Letters, Poetry Northwest, Kentucky Poetry Review* and *Cimarron Review.*

ELIZABETH HAZEN received an M.A. from the Writing Seminars at Johns Hopkins University. Her poems have appeared in *Wordwrights!, Hanging Loose,* and *Nimrod.* The Argonne House Press has published two of her chapbooks.

WILLIAM HEATH, Professor of English at Mount Saint Mary's College, Emmitsburg, Maryland, is the author of a book of poems, *The Walking Man* (Icarus, 1994) and an award-winning novel about the civil rights movement in Mississippi, *The Children Bob Moses Led* (Milkweed Editions, 1995).

CHERYL HELLNER's most recent poems have appeared in *Peregrine, Wild Earth* and *Heron Dance.* She is a teacher as well as a poet.

MARY HILTON lives in Washington, D.C. Her work has appeared in *So to Speak, Washington Review, apex of the M, Poetics Briefs, lower limit speech,* and *Texture.* Her chapbook, *Fool Savior* was published by Texture Press. She is the founding editor of primitive publications, a press dedicated to historically influenced literature.

ERICH HINTZE is an electronic commerce negotiator, adjunct Professor of English at the College of Southern Maryland, and serves as a reader judge for The Edgar Allan Poe Poetry Memorial and The Washington Prize. His first book, *Blue Magic Straw,* is scheduled for publication in 2003.

CYNTHIA MARIE HOFFMAN is the founding editor of *Frantic Egg,* a biannual mini-journal of poetry. Her work has appeared in *Poet Lore, Gargoyle, Rattle,* and *Phoebe.* She has studied literature in St. Petersburg, Russia, and received an M.F.A from George Mason University.

JAMES C. HOPKINS has received two Jenny McKean Moore scholarships (George Washington University), and has acted as co-director of The Word Works Washington Prize. He has published a chapbook, *The Walnut Tree Waits For Its Bees* (Mica Press), and *eight pale women,* a collection of poetry (The Word Works Capital Collection, 2003).

PAUL HOPPER, formerly a teacher of German and related subjects, has been a translator for the federal government since 1981. His poems and translations have appeared in *Texas Quarterly, Pivot,* and *The Federal Poet.* He used to write reviews of Norwegian fiction and poetry for *Books Abroad,* which became *World Literature Today.*

JOANNA HOWARD teaches at Montgomery College-Rockville where she coordinates Developmental Writing. She is currently pursuing an M.A. in writing at Johns Hopkins University.

BERT HUBINGER holds a B.A. from Dartmouth and an M.A. from Catholic University. He has worked as an editor, teacher, copywriter and magazine research writer. His book, *Sea Drums & Other Poems* (Eastwind, 2003) was recently published.

REUBEN JACKSON, an archivist for the Smithsonian, also writes music reviews. His book of poems, *Fingering the Keys,* won the Columbia Book Award, chosen by Joseph Brodsky, and his poems have been anthologized in *Our Souls Have Grown Deep Like the Rivers: Black Poets Read Their Work.*

BRUCE A. JACOBS is the author of *Speaking Through My Skin* (Michigan State University Press), which won the Naomi Long Madgett Poetry Prize, and the nonfiction book, *Race Manners: Navigating the Minefield Between Black and White Americans* (Arcade). He has had residences at MacDowell and at the Ucross Foundation. He lives in Baltimore.

ROY JACOBSTEIN, a physician and former USAID official, received the Randall Jarrell Prize for his chapbook, *Blue Numbers, Red Life.* He was nominated for a Pushcart Prize, was a finalist for the Academy of American Poets' Walt Whitman Award, and won the 2002 Felix Pollak Prize from the University of Wisconsin Press for his book, *Ripe.*

VALERIE JEAN is a poet/musician. She combines her two loves in a mix/mess she calls flu-oetry. She is also an editor and a teacher who currently teaches creative writing at the University of Maryland and conducts a community creative writing workshop.

ROD JELLEMA, Professor Emeritus at the University of Maryland, has recently published poems in *Field, Plum Review, Nimrod, Christian Century, Image, Atlanta Review,* and *Many Mountains Moving.* Born and raised on the shores of Lake Michigan, he and his wife spend about half of each year in Old San Juan, Puerto Rico.

BRANDON D. JOHNSON is a Larry Neal Writers' Competition award winner, a former Cave Canem Fellow, and a D.C. Commission on the Arts and Humanities grant recipient. His work has appeared in *The Drumming Between Us, Fodderwing, Callaloo,* and elsewhere. He is the author of *The Strangers Between* and *Man Burns Ant.*

JEAN H. JOHNSON's book of poems is *Forgotten Alphabet* (SCOP Publications, 1994), and her work has appeared in *Poet Lore, Larcom Review, Hampton-Sydney Review,* and elsewhere.

NANCY JOHNSON is the author of a collection of poems, *Zoo & Cathedral* (1996), which won the 1995 White Pine Press Poetry Prize. She is currently at work on a non-fiction book about the conjunction of her son's cystic fibrosis and her own marathon training. She lives in Oakland, California, with her husband and son.

ANN RAE JONAS' poetry has appeared in *Hanging Loose, Dreamworks, Crosscurrents, River City, Frank, The G.W. Review, Artful Dodge,* and *Seneca Review.* Her book of poetry, *A Diamond Is Hard but Not Tough* (The Word Works, 1997) won the Washington Prize. She lives in New York City.

BETH BARUCH JOSELOW is the author of six books of poetry and a book of exercises for writers, *Writing Without the Muse.* She teaches at the Corcoran College of Art and Design in Washington, D.C.

MIRIAM KESSLER, mother of four and grandmother of six, has given poetry readings in many states, has read her work on WITF-FM, National Public Radio, and conducts poetry and prose readings at a local library.

SALLY ROSEN KINDRED received her B.A. from Duke and her M.F.A. from the University of Maryland. Her poems have appeared in *Poetry Northwest, Poet Lore, Earth's Daughters,* and *The Baltimore Review*, and are forthcoming in *Small Pond.*

THOMAS M. KIRLIN won the Larry Neal Award a decade ago. His poems appear in *Hungry As We Are* (Washington Writers' Publishing House, 1995) and other anthologies, and he co-authored with his wife the *Smithsonian Folklife Cookbook.* He holds a Ph.D. in English Literature and has taught at the University of Wisconsin-Madison.

WAYNE KLINE lives a secluded life in Manassas, Virginia. He reports that his days are rather special.

ANN B. KNOX has two books of poetry, *Staying is Nowhere*, winner of the Writer's Center/SCOP Publishing Prize; *Stonecrop,* (Washington Writers' Publishing House); and a collection of short stories. She has been editor of *Antietam Review* for 20 years.

LISA KOSOW's poems have appeared in *Gargoyle, The Connecticut River Review, Wordwrights!, Potpourri, The Plastic Tower* and *Perceptions*, and in her chapbook, *Dawn is Moving* (Argonne House Press). She lives in Takoma Park, Maryland.

CAROLYN KREITER-FORONDA has published four poetry books and co-edited a poetry anthology. Her poems have appeared in *Prairie Schooner, Mid-American Review, Antioch Review,* and *Poet Lore,* among others. Her numerous grants and awards include three Artist-in-Education grants from The Virginia Commission for the Arts.

DAVID KRESH is a Reference Specialist in Poetry at the Library of Congress and Poet-in-Residence at the Capitol Hill Day School. His poems have appeared in two books, *Bloody Joy: Love Poems* (Slow Dancer, 1981) and *Sketches After "Pete's Beer"* (Stone Man, 1986). He has been an editor for the British magazine and press, *Slow Dancer.*

CABIN FEVER--

Robert Krut's work has appeared in *The American Literary Review, Many Mountains Moving, Zone 3, Sundog, The Southeast Review,* and *Whiskey Island,* among others. He holds an M.F.A. from Arizona State University where he received two Swarthout Awards in writing. He currently teaches at Georgia State University.

KwelismitH is the author of *Secret Meeting Kawanzaa Songs and City Sounds* (Book/CD). She has presented her interdisciplinary performance art, combining music, poetry, movement and visual art at such diverse venues as Johns Hopkins University, The Black Arts Festival in Atlanta, George Mason University and Oberlin College.

Hiram Larew's poems have appeared in 80 small journals including *The Bellingham Review, The Antietam Review, SpoonFed,* and *The Great Lawn.* He reads his work widely and has won regional prizes, including Baltimore's ARTSCAPE Poetry Prize and the *Louisiana Literature* Poetry Award. He is one of the tallest poets writing today.

Merrill Leffler has published two collections of poems, *Partly Pandemonium, Partly Love* and *Take Hold* and edited *The Changing Orders: Poetry from Israel,* a special edition of *Poet Lore* (1986). A new collection, *Mark the Music,* is planned for 2003. Leffler is the publisher of Dryad Press in Maryland.

Jeffrey Levine's collection of poems, *Mortal Everlasting* (Pavement Saw Press, 2002) won the Transcontinental Poetry Award.

Vladimir Levchev, born in Bulgaria where he has published 15 books of poetry, essays and fiction, now lives in Washington, D.C. His American books of poetry include *Leaves from the Dry Tree* (Cross-Cultural Communications, N.Y., 1996, translated by Henry Taylor), and *Black Book of the Endangered Species* (The Word Works, 1999).

Lenny Lianne is a poet and artist living in Ramona, California. Her poems recently have appeared in the anthology, *Driftwood Highway,* and in *Tidepools.* Her drawings have graced several covers of *Friendly Woman.*

M.L. Liebler is the author of several books, including the *2000 Written in Rain: New & Selected Poems* (Tebot Bach Books) which received the Wayne State University Board of Governors Book Award. He has also released two CDs of music and poetry with The Magic Poetry Band and Country Joe McDonald. He teaches at Wayne State University.

Toni Asante Lightfoot, poet, activist and organizer, has been a teacher at Duke Ellington School of the Arts as well as with the Writers Corps. She left Washington, D.C., in 2000 to start a bed & breakfast in Trinidad & Tobago. She now lives in Chicago.

Gary Lilley, born and raised in Sandy Cross, North Carolina, received two D.C. Commission on the Arts Fellowships for Poetry in 1996 and 2000 and is currently a student in the Warren Wilson College M.F.A. Program for Writers.

Chris Llewellyn is an instructor of poetry at The Writer's Center and has served in WritersCorps/AmeriCorps. She earned an M.F.A. in Creative Writing from Warren Wilson College. Her poetry books are *Fragments From the Fire* (Walt Whitman Award, Penguin, 1987) and *Steam Dummy* (Bottom Dog Press,1993).

Carmen Lupton, a freelance writer and editor, and literacy advocate, has taught poetry, literature and reading, and worked as a voice-over artist. Her poetry has been published in *The Provincetown Paper, Boston Reader, Cathay, Hungry as We Are: An Anthology of Washington Area Poets* (Washington Writers' Publishing House), and *Mondo Barbie* (St. Martin's Press).

Elaine Magarrell, a retired writer and teacher, has published two books of poetry: *On Hogback Mountain* (Washington Writers' Publishing House) and *Blameless Lives* (The Word Works). She lives in Washington, D.C., with her husband and travels extensively.

Dora Malech is an M.F.A. candidate in the Iowa Writers' Workshop. Her work has appeared in *Poetry Northwest, Gargoyle,*

Hayden's Ferry Review and in her chapbook, *Inside and Elsewhere* (Argonne House Press).

Fred Marchant's first book, *Tipping Point* (The Word Works), won the 1993 Washington Prize, and his second book, *Full Moon Boat* (Graywolf Press) was recently published. He is a Professor of English and Director of the Creative Writing Program at Suffolk University in Boston and serves on the Executive Board of PEN New England.

Sydney March, a native of Kingston, Jamaica, has won numerous prizes for his poetry. His work includes *Stealing Mangoes*, a chapbook from Mica Press.

David McAleavey has taught at George Washington University since 1974. His first three books of poems were published by Ithaca House in 1971, 1975 and 1980. His more recent books are *Holding Obsidian* (Washington Writers' Publishing House, 1985), and *Greatest Hits 1971-2000* (Pudding House Publications, 2001). *Huge Haiku* (Chax Press) is due to be published in 2003.

Maia McAleavey is a senior English Major at Stanford University where she won the Urmy-Hardy Poetry Prize for best undergraduate poem in 2001. While a senior at Yorktown High School, locally, she won The Word Works Young Poets Competition.

Greg McBride, an attorney at the U.S. Department of Transportation, has work published or forthcoming in *Potomac Review, Gettysburg Review* and *Poet Lore.*

Richard McCann is the author of *Ghost Letters* and the co-editor of *Things Shaped in Passing: More 'Poets for Life' Writing from the AIDS Pandemic.* He has published fiction, poetry and creative nonfiction in *The Atlantic, Esquire, Tin House,* and in numerous anthologies. He teaches at American University.

Judith McCombs has three collections of poetry: *Against Nature: Wilderness Poems* (Dustbooks); *Sisters & Other Selves* (Glass Bell); and *Territories, Here & Elsewhere* (Mayapple). Her work has appeared in *Calyx, Nimrod* (Pablo Neruda Award), *Poet Lore, Poetry, Poetry Northwest, Potomac Review* (Poetry Prize), *Prairie Schooner,* and others.

Craig McEldowney lives in New York City where he has several projects underway, including a chapbook, a spoken-word CD, and improvised music. He has participated in poetry readings/slams at Urbana and the Nuyorican Poet's Café.

James McEuen's poems have appeared in *Poetry Northwest, Prairie Schooner, Poet Lore, The Maryland Poetry Review,* among others. His book, *Snake Country,* was The Word Works' selection for the 1990 Capital Collection.

E. Ethelbert Miller is the author of *Fathering Words: The Making of An African American Writer.* He is a founding member of the Humanities Council of Washington, D.C., a Commissioner for the D.C. Commission on the Arts and Humanities, and an editor of *Poet Lore.*

Larry Moffi is the author of three collections of poems and three non-fiction books on baseball.

Gary Moody has published poems in *The Carolina Literary Companion, AKROS, Au Verso, So to Speak,* and *Phoebe*. He holds an M.F.A. from George Mason University.

David Moolten's poems have appeared in such journals as *The Sewanee Review, The Southern Review* and *Poetry.* His first book, *Plums & Ashes* (1994) won the Samuel French Morse Poetry Prize. A practicing physician, Dr. Moolten lives in Philadelphia.

Miles David Moore is the author of *The Bears of Paris* (The Word Works Capital Collection, 1995) and *Buddha Isn't Laughing* (Argonne House Press, 1999). He co-edited *Winners: A Retrospective of the Washington Prize* (The Word Works, 1999). He has won many literary prizes. such as the Rose Lefcowitz Essay Prize (*Poet Lore*) and the *Potomac Review* Poetry Prize.

Miriam Mörsel Nathan's work has appeared in *Gargoyle, Arts & Letters: Journal of Contemporary Culture* and the anthologies *Daughters of Absence* (Capital Books, Inc.) and *From Daughters & Sons*

CABIN FEVER--

to Fathers: What I've Never Said (Story Line Press). Recently, she was awarded a fellowship by the Virginia Center for the Creative Arts.

FAYE MOSKOWITZ, English Department chair at George Washington University, is author of *A Leak in the Heart; Whoever Finds This: I Love You; And the Bridge is Love; Peace in the House* (forthcoming) and editor of *Her Face in the Mirror: Jewish Women on Mothers and Daughters.*

KERMIT MOYER is a co-director of the M.F.A. Program in Creative Writing at American University. His poems and stories have appeared in *Pulpsmith, Cumberland Poetry Review, Tendril, The Georgia Review, The Southern Review, The Sewanee Review,* and *The Hudson Review.* He is the author of a collection of stories entitled *Tumbling* (University of Illinois, 1988).

SHARON NEGRI's poems have appeared in several journals, three anthologies, in her chapbook, *Ruby And Other Lives* (Argonne House Press), and in her book, *The Other Side Of Now* (Washington Writers' Publishing House, 1989). She is currently at work on her next collection.

LYUBOMIR NIKOLOV was born in the Bulgarian village of Kiryaevo but has lived in the U.S. since 1990. His latest collection of poetry, *Raven*, was published in Sofia in 1995.

MARY HAYNE NORTH lives on a river in the Blue Ridge Mountains and works as a school board member while pursuing studies through the New England School of Homeopathy. She was the first recipient of the Virginia Prize for Poetry and has been a Fellow at Virginia Center for Creative Arts. Her poetry has appeared in *Arts Alive 2000.*

SIBBIE O'SULLIVAN lives and writes in Wheaton, Maryland.

MICHELLE PARKERSON is a performance poet, independent filmmaker and Assistant Professor at Temple University's Department of Film & Media Arts. Her work appears in several journals and anthologies including *Gargoyle 37 / 38; In Search of Color Everywhere; Fast Talk, Full Volume* and *The Arc of Love.*

ALICIA PARTNOY, a survivor of the secret detention camps where about 30,000 Argentineans "disappeared," authored *The Little School: Tales of Disappearance and Survival, Revenge of the Apple—Venganza de la Manzana,* and edited *You Can't Drown the Fire.* She teaches at Loyola Marymount University in Los Angeles.

MARIE PAVLICEK-WEHRLI's poems have appeared in various literary magazines and anthologies, including *The Beloit Poetry Journal* and *Hungry as We Are: An Anthology of Washington Area Poets* (Washington Writers' Publishing House, 1995). A painter, she received a Virginia Center for the Creative Arts fellowship in 2000 and now lives in Silver Spring, Maryland.

PATRIC PEPPER lives in Washington DC. His poetry has appeared in various magazines: *WordWrights!, Medicinal Purposes, Blue Unicorn, Pivot, The Edge City Review, ELF, The Comstock Review* and others. His chapbook, *Zoned Industrial,* won the Annual *Medicinal Purposes* Chapbook Contest in 2000.

ARLENE PLEVIN has published in *The Literature of Nature: An International Sourcebook,* and *Bicycling* magazine. Her books include one on bicycling. She has an M.F.A. in poetry from Iowa, an English Ph.D. from the University of Washington, and received a Fulbright Scholarship to teach and study in Taiwan.

KATHERINE PLIMPTON is a student at George Mason University majoring in English with a concentration in poetry.

STANLEY PLUMLY, a Distinguished Professor of English at the University of Maryland, has won numerous awards for his poetry. His most recent book, *Now That My Father Lies Down Beside Me: New and Selected Poems* was published in 2000 (Ecco Press).

JACKLYN W. POTTER has published poems in journals such as *Plainsong, Hollins Critic,* and *Poet Lore*, and in anthologies such as *If I Had My Life to Live Over, I'd Pick More Daisies*, and *Weavings 2000, The Maryland Millennial Anthology*. She has published translation work in *The Washington Review, Stone Country* and *Delos*. She has received four grants from the D.C. Commission on the Arts.

MINNIE BRUCE PRATT's most recent book of poetry, *Walking Back Up Depot Street,* was named the year's Best Lesbian/Gay Book by *ForeWord: Magazine of Independent Bookstores and Booksellers.* Her second book, *Crime Against Nature* (1989), was a Lamont Poetry Selection of the Academy of American Poets.

MARY QUATTLEBAUM is the author of ten children's books, most recently *Grover G. Graham and Me, The Shine Man,* and *Underground Train*. She has received the Marguerite de Angeli Prize, the Sugarman Award, Parenting Reading Magic Award, and other honors.

LUIS REBAZA-SORALUZ teaches Latin American literature and visual arts at King's College, University of London. He has authored three books of poetry, *Población activa* (1978), *Hipervivientes* (1980) and *Del reino y la frontera* (1985, 1992).

ELIZABETH REES' poetry has appeared in *Partisan Review, Kenyon Review, Agni, Southern Poetry Review, Seneca Review* and other journals. Her chapbook, *Balancing China* (1999), won the Sow's Ear Press' national contest. She studied with George Starbuck and Derek Walcott at Boston University.

MICHAEL REINKE was born in western New York State and currently resides with his wife and daughter in Lexington, Kentucky. His poetry and stories have appeared in a variety of journals and reviews, and he is the author of two poetry chapbooks. In 1996, he founded and coordinated the Glenview Mansion poetry series in Rockville, Maryland.

MICHAEL REIS has had poems published in *Gargoyle, Unicorn, Urthkin, Lucille,* and *Amelia* (Postcard Series, 1985). An environmental historian, he has read his poetry from Baltimore to New Jersey and devoutly wishes never to recover from cabin fever.

SUZANNE RHODENBAUGH's book *Lick of Sense* (Helicon Nine Editions, 2001) won the Marianne Moore Poetry Prize. Formerly a resident in the Washington metropolitan area, she now lives in St. Louis. Her poems have appeared widely in journals, in several anthologies, and in four chapbooks.

DWAINE RIEVES is a physician in the Public Health Service. His poems have appeared in *The Georgia Review, River Styx* and *Chelsea*.

MAY RIHANI, a Lebanese-American poet, has published three collections: *Engraving on the Days* (1969); *My Name Is the Other* (1974); and *...It Encircles the Waist of the Earth* (1993). As an international education development professional, she travels often to Africa and the Middle East to work with governments on educational reforms.

HUGO RIZZOLI lives in Royal Oak, Maryland. The author of *Cape Strata* (Sedwick House, 1989), he is at work on a series of poems about the Chesapeake Bay.

KIM ROBERTS is the author of a book of poems, *The Wishbone Galaxy* (Washington Writers' Publishing House). She has received grants from the National Endowment of the Humanities, the D.C. Commission on the Arts, and residency grants from ten artist colonies. She edits *Beltway: An On-Line Poetry Quarterly.*

JAY ROGOFF is the author of two books of poetry, *The Cutoff* (The Word Works, 1995), and *How We Came to Stand on That Shore* (River City, 2003), and a chapbook, *First Hand* (Mica, 1997). His poems and criticism appear in many journals, and he teaches at Skidmore College in its Liberal Studies Program.

MAGGIE ROSEN, from Greensboro, North Carolina, currently resides in Silver Spring, Maryland. Her poems have appeared in *Sow's Ear, Minimus, Plainsong, Lonzie's Fried Chicken,* and the anthologies *Hungry As We Are: An Anthology of Washington Area Poets* (Washington Writers' Publishing House, 1995) and *Winners: A Retrospective of the Washington Prize* (The Word Works, 1999).

AMY JO ROSS lives and works in Washington, D.C. Her poems have appeared in *Poet Lore, Visions International, Potomac Review, Winners: A Retrospective of the Washington Prize* (The Word

Works, 1999), and are forthcoming online at *InPosse Review.*

Martha Sanchez-Lowery is the poetry editor of *Minimus* and former director of The Word Works Washington Prize. Her chapbook is *Bocanegra* (Mica, 1997). Her work has appeared in The *Hispanic Culture Review,* Anaya Press. Her poetry was displayed on Arlington buses as part of the Moving Words Series X, and on the e-zine *Beltway*.

Robert Sargent is the author of nine books of poetry and two chapbooks, the most recent being *Wondrous News: The Biblical Poems* (2001). He is an honorary Board Member of the The Word Works and of The Bunny and Crocodile Press, and he received the 1996 Columbia Merit Award.

M. A. Schaffner has poems published or forthcoming in *Prairie Schooner, Imago* (Australia), *Orbis* (UK), *Poetry Salzburg,* and *Abiko Annual* (Japan). His book, *The Good Opinion of Squirrels* (The Word Works, 1996), won the Writer's Center publication prize and the Columbia Book Award.

Janice Lynch Schuster is a graduate of the M.F.A. program at American University. She writes full-time about end-of-life issues. She lives in Annapolis with her six children.

Myra Shapiro's first poetry collection, *I'll See You Thursday* (Blue Sofa Press, 1996), was edited by Robert Bly. Her poems have appeared in *The Harvard Review, The Ohio Review,* and *The Best American Poetry 1999* and *2003* (Scribner). She was awarded The New School's Dylan Thomas Poetry Award.

Anne Sheldon is a lecturer at the University of Maryland and a poet-in-the-schools. Her work has appeared in *Poet Lore, Antietam Review, Weird Tales, Phoebe* and *Dreams of Decadence*. The Word Works published her chapbook, *Lancastrian Letters,* in 1997.

Shan Shi is an aspiring writer and performer who has received several literary, theatrical, and academic honors, and has held a student fellowship at the Folger Shakespeare Research Library. Her theatre training is from the University of Southern California.

Thandiwe Shiphrah is a poet and performance artist originally from Washington, D.C. She recently completed a full-length manuscript of poems entitled, *Leftover Light,* and the spoken-word CD, *The Secret Marvelous Instead.*

Enid Shomer is the author of four poetry books, most recently *Stars at Noon: Poems from the Life of Jacqueline Cochran* (U. Arkansas), and of *Imaginary Men,* which won the Iowa Fiction Prize and the Louisiana State University/ Southern Review Prize. Her work has appeared in *The New Yorker, Atlantic,* and *The Paris Review.*

Askold Skalsky's poetry has been published in numerous small press magazines including *Southern Poetry Review, Waterstone, Northeast Corridor,* and *Borderlands*. He has also published in Canada, Ireland, and Great Britain.

Myra Sklarew, a professor at American University, is the author of nine poetry collections including *Lithuania: New and Selected Poems* (Azul Editions, 1995), and *Over the Rooftops of Time,* essays, 2003. She is currently at work on a nonfiction book, *Holocaust and the Construction of Memory.*

J.D. Smith's publications include the collection *The Hypothetical Landscape* (Quarterly Review of Literature, 1999) and the anthology *Northern Music: Poems About and Inspired by Glenn Gould*. He also writes and publishes fiction, essays, drama and reviews.

Rose Solari's honors include the Randall Jarrell Poetry Prize, an Academy of American Poets' University Prize and the Columbia Book Award for *Difficult Weather* (Gut Punch Press, 1994). She has also published two chapbooks. *The Stolen World* (ARTSCAPE, 1993) and *Selections from Myths and Elegies* (Argonne House Press, 1999).

Susan Sonde's second collection of poetry, *In the Longboats with Others* (New Rivers Press) won the Capricorn Book Award. She was the recipient of Maryland State Arts Grants for poetry and fiction. Her short stories have appeared in such journals as *Quarterly West* and *Carolina Quarterly.* Her poems have appeared in *Southern Humanities Review* and many other magazines. She is finishing a novel.

DAVID SOSNOWSKI has worked as a teacher, editor, gag writer, fireworks salesman, and bureaucrat in Detroit, D.C., and Fairbanks. His work has appeared in numerous literary magazines. His first novel, *Rapture* (Random House,1996), garnered popular and critical acclaim in the U.S. and the U.K. He is currently working on his second novel.

GARY STEIN's poems have appeared in *Poetry, Poet Lore, Prairie Schooner, Folio, Wind, JAMA, WordWrights!, The Antietam Review*, and elsewhere. He has taught poetry writing in colleges and high schools, holds an M.F.A. from the University of Iowa, and currently is the book review editor for *Poet Lore.* He practices law in Washington, D.C.

SARAH STILLMAN, a student at Yale, is the author of *Soul Searching: A Girl's Guide to Finding Herself.* She received the Parkmont Poetry Prize and the The Word Works Young Poets Award.

SILVANA STRAW's solo performance, *Scared of Myself: the Return of Uncle Silvana,* commissioned by The Washington Performing Arts Society, premiered at Dance Place in 2000. As Poetry Slam Champion, she represented D.C. at the National Slam in '93-'94. She has won the Larry Neal Writer's Award and has published in *The Indiana Review.*

THOM STUART's work appears or is forthcoming in *Live Poets Anthology, WordWrights!, Potomac Review, Curbside Review, Peralta Press, Freshwater, Small Brushes,* and *Anthology*. He won First Prize in the 2002 Poetry Society of Virginia contest.

ROBIN SULEIMAN has published fiction, poetry and plays in such places as *The Susquehanna Review* and *Visions International.* Currently at work on his second novel, he lives with his wife and dog in New Hope, Pennsylvania, where he works as a freelance writer and presentation consultant.

ELIZABETH SULLAM, born in Italy, now lives in Washington where she has taught at the Johns Hopkins School of Advanced International Studies. She published *Out of Bound* (Catholic University Press), a collection of poems. Her historical novel, *A Canosa,* published in Italy, won the Presidential Award and the Premio Lunigiana.

TERESE SVOBODA's most recent book of poetry is *Treason.* Her most recent prose book is *Trailer Girl and Other Stories.* She has taught at William and Mary, Williams, and Sarah Lawrence.

JOSEPH THACKERY, eighty-nine years old, is a retired labor lawyer with many appearances in magazines and journals. His book of poems, *The Dark Above Mad River* was published by Washington Writers' Publishing House (1992). He still hosts "The Ellicott Poets" in alternating months.

HILARY THAM, author of nine books of poetry and a memoir, is the editor-in-chief for The Word Works and poetry editor for *Potomac Review.* She teaches creative writing and has received many grants from the Virginia Commission for the Arts.

NAOMI THIERS is a reading specialist and writing teacher at Montessori School of McLean. Her first book was *Only the Raw Hands Are Heaven* (Washington Writers' Publishing House, 1992).

COLETTE THOMAS's poems have appeared in *Grand Street, Poet Lore*, and elsewhere. She has presented her poetry at the Library of Congress, the Folger Shakespeare Library, and Harvard University (where she studied with Seamus Heaney). She is a long-time student of the I Ching and teaches Taoist meditation.

JONATHAN VAILE, a two-time NEH grant winner and a former member of the D.C. National Slam Team, has been published in *Phoebe, Poet Lore, Exquisite Corpse, Minimus* and *Winners: A Retrospective of The Washington Prize* (The Word Works, 1999). He lives in Alexandria with his wife and their dog.

MICHAEL VARGA retired from the U.S. Foreign Service in 1996. His short story,

"Collapsing Into Zimbabwe," won first prize in *The Toronto Star*'s annual competition. He recently completed a novel and resides in Cape May, New Jersey.

DAVI WALDERS is a writer and education consultant whose work appears in numerous journals, newspapers, and anthologies. Her latest poetry collection, *Gifts*, was commissioned by the Milton Murray Foundation. She developed and directs the Vital Signs Poetry Project at the National Institutes of Health and its Children's Inn.

MARK WALLACE has published several collections of poems. *Temporary Worker Rides A Subway* (Sun and Moon, forthcoming) won the New American Poetry Award. With Steven Marks, he co-edited the essay collection *Telling It Slant: Avant-Garde Poetics of the 1990s* (University of Alabama Press, 2001).

BARRETT WARNER's work can be seen in *Gargoyle, Smartish Pace, Baltimore Review, Comstock Review* and *Roanoke Review*. His chapbook *'Til I'm Blue in the Face* (Tropos) appeared in 1996. Barrett is a horseman working at Pimlico Race Track and several local farms.

CHARLOTTE GOULD WARREN's book, *Gandhi's Lap* (The Word Works, 2000), won the Washington Prize. Her poems have appeared on Seattle's buses and in *The Literary Review, Southern Poetry Review,* and *Kansas Quarterly*. She received an M.F.A. from Vermont College and teaches college English part-time.

DEBORAH WASSERTZUG won the Young Poets Competition in 1989. Since 1998 she has lived in New York City, where she works as a librarian and writes poetry. Her work has appeared on the website, *can we have our ball back?*

MICHAEL WATERS teaches at Salisbury University in Maryland and is the author of *Parthenopi: New and Selected Poems* (BOA Editions, 2001). He has also edited (with the late A. Poulin, Jr.) *Contemporary American Poetry* (Houghton Mifflin, 2001) and is the recipient of a Fellowship in Poetry from the National Endowment for the Arts.

MARGARET WEAVER, a retired tree farmer and high school English teacher, has published poems in *Yankee, Poetry Northwest, Poet Lore,* and other journals. Her first book was *Escaping Words* (Washington Writers' Publishing House, 2001).

ERICA WEITZMAN received an M.F.A. in Creative Writing from Boston University, graduating with the Hurley Memorial Prize for poetry. Recently she lived in Gjakova, Kosovo, and worked for Balkan Sunflowers, a humanitarian aid organization. She now resides in New York where she graduated from New School University.

PHILIP WEXLER lives and works in Bethesda, Maryland. He has published some 60 poems in magazines over the years, including *The Baltimore Review* and *Wavelength*.

REED WHITTEMORE has written numerous books since publication of his first book, *Heroes and Heroines* (Reynal and Hitchcock, 1946). He has served as Poet Laureate for the State of Maryland and is currently a Professor of English at the University of Maryland.

RHONDA WILLIFORD, a lawyer for the National Labor Relations Board, has published poems in *Plum Review, Wordwrights!, Folio, Bellowing Ark, Beauty for Ashes,* and in the on-line journal, *Beltway*. Her chapbook is *One Wide Sky* (Argonne Hotel, 1997).

MARY-SHERMAN WILLIS has published poems and reviews in *The New Republic, Poet Lore, Plum Review,* and elsewhere. A Washington native, she is enrolled in the M.F.A. program at Warren Wilson College.

RONALD WILSON is a native of Takoma Park, Maryland.

TERENCE WINCH's most recent book is *The Drift of Things* (The Figures, 2001). His work has appeared widely in such publications as *The Paris Review, Verse,* and *The American Poetry Review*. He has received an N.E.A poetry fellowship and an American Book Award for *Irish Musicians/American Friends* (Coffee House, 1986).

David Wolinsky claims to have written an unpublished five-slim-volume work of poetry, collectively titled, *The Tomb of the Unknown Holder.* He lives in Maryland and teaches reading to troubled, troubling, amazing kids.

Anne Harding Woodworth's poetry has appeared in *U.S. Catholic, Cimarron Review, Painted Bride Quarterly, Potomac Review,* and elsewhere. Her four years in Greece helped inspire her chapbook, *Aesop's Eagles and Poems from the Road* (Northwoods, 2001). Her most recent book is *The Mushroom Papers* (Northwoods, 2002).

George Young is a physician practicing in Boulder, Colorado. His book, *Spinoza's Mouse* (The Word Works, 1996), won the Washington Prize. He has published a chapbook, *Creating The Universe* (Perivale Press, 1996), and his poems have appeared in two anthologies of poems by doctors, *Blood & Bone* and *Uncharted Lines.*

Others Who Read in the Series

1984 - 1989

Julia Watson Barbour
Carrington Bonner
Rocky Curtis
Toi Derricotte
Cornelius Eady
Alice Foster
Andrew Grossman
Pat Hutchings
Delores Kendrick
Diana Linkous
Ron Morgan
Gregory Orfalea
David Price-Gresty
Catherine Harnett Shaw
Toni Stewart
Garth Tate
Dale Williams

Marguerite Beck-Rex
Robert Bowie
Ann Darr
Tamara Dietrich
Laura Flippin
William H. Green
Judith Harris
Jacquie Jones
Helga Kopperl
D. Milowe
Fortune Rebecca Nagle
Betty Parry
Lisa Ress
Deborah Snyder
Linda Stiles
Reetika Vazirani
Kirk Wilson

1990 - 1995

Michael Albo
Cristina Brown
Lisa Cantey
Caleb Corkery
Jennifer Dante
Elisabeth Enagonio
Phillis Levin
Sara Levy
Kim Linn
Tom Mandel
Tracee Rhodes
Georgia Scott
Natasha Tarpley
Belle Waring
Nancy White

Agha Shahid Ali
Moira Burns
Guang-Shing Cheng
Ruth Coyne
Sarah DeWeerdt
Jim Henley
Melissa Levine
Melvin Lewis
Jon Loomis
W. Dale Nelson
Joe Ross
Ann Strom
Sue Teigen
Sonja Weisel

1996 - 2001

Joe Bawol
Nancy Galbraith
Stephen Hester
Jennifer LeRoy
Melissa Marshall
Lisa Parker
Frank Sherlock
Lyrae Van Clief-Stefanon
Seshat Yon'shea

Linda Jay Burke
A. C. Gavis
Susan Landers
Caroline Marshall
Shuja Nawaz
Joan Retallack
Damon Talbott
Gabriele Priska Von Beroldingen

Acknowledgments

The editors are grateful to the poets and copyright owners for permission to include their poems in the Anthology.

ALLY ACKER: "White Noise At Midnight" was first published in her book, *Surviving Desire*, Garden Street Press, 1994.

KARREN L. ALENIER: "Something Growing" was first published in *The Frantic Egg*, August, 2000.

ELIZABETH ALEXANDER: "Peccant" was originally published in *Antebellum Dream Book*, Graywolf Press, 2001.

NATHALIE ANDERSON: "Juke Box Memories" and "Cold Sweat" were first published in her Washington Prize-winning book, *Following Fred Astaire,* The Word Works, 1998.

BARRI ARMITAGE: "Square Dance" is from her book, *Double Helix,* Washington Writers' Publishing House, 1993, and first appeared in *The Georgia Review,* 1984. It was reprinted in *Anthology of Magazine Verse and Yearbook of American Poetry, 1985,* and *American Squaredance*, 1988. "Fall Ritual" is from *Double Helix,* Washington Writers' Publishing House, 1993. The poem was first published in *Poetry*, September, 1986, and was reprinted in *Out of Season,* The Amagansett Press, 1993.

RENÉE ASHLEY: "Obsolete Angel" was published in her book, *The Various Reasons of Light,* Avocet Press, 1998, and first appeared in *Sycamore Review.*

JENNIFER ATKINSON: "Three Years: a Composition in Gesso and Graphite" was first published in her book, *The Drowned City,* Northeastern University Press, 2000.

NED BALBO: "Red Planet" was first published in his book, *Galileo's Banquet,* Washington Writers' Publishing House, 1998.

HOLLY BASS: "gleam" was first published in *Callaloo*, Fall, 1999.

MEL BELIN: "Webs" was first published in *Flesh That Was Chrysallis,* The Word Works, 1999.

PETER BLAIR: "The Night We Pitch It" was first published in his Washington Prize-winning book, *Last Heat,* The Word Works, 2000.

ANNE MARIE BLUM: "Scars" was previously published in *Rattapallax*, Issue 3, 2000.

JOHN BRADLEY: "Where I Live" was first published in *College English,* January, 1995.

DORIS BRODY: "Place of the Turtles Bay" was first published in her book, *Judging the Distance,* The Word Works, 2001.

RICK CANNON: "Point of Arrival" was first published in *Poet Lore,* 1996.

NANCY NAOMI CARLSON: "What Cannot Be Held" was first published in *Poetry*, 1999.

GRACE CAVALIERI: "The Liberation of Music" was first published in *The Jazz Poetry Anthology,* Sascha Feinstein & Yusef Komunyakaa, Editors, Indiana University Press, December, 1996.

LUCILLE CLIFTON: "homage to my hips" is from her book *Two Headed Woman,* University of Massachusetts Press, 1980.

SHIRLEY COCHRANE: "View as Art" is from *The Cape Rock,* 2001.

DON COLBURN: "Wildflowers" first appeared in *The Nation,* 1993.

MICHAEL COLLIER: "The Barber" was previously published in his collection, *The Neighbor,* University of Chicago Press, 1995.

ANDREA COLLINS: "After the Second Night of Your First Ob/Gyn Rotation" first appeared in *Northeast Journal,* 1991.

Sarah Cotterill: "You Filed in the Oldest Paths" was first published in *The Ohio Review*, 1996.

Lois Cucullu: "Breathing Space" was first published in *Uncommon Place: An Anthology of Contemporary Louisiana Poets,* Louisiana State University Press, 1998.

Enid Dame: "Lot's Wife" was first published in *On the Road to Damascus, Maryland,* Downtown Poets, N.Y., 1980.

Michael C. Davis: "Hunger" was first published in *Minimus,* Vol. 8, 1998.

Sean Enright: "Anger" was first published in *Southern Poetry Review,* 1998, and "Spiderman" was first published in *Tikkun*, 2001.

Doug Evans: "Sonnet Written in Snow" was first published in *Frantic Egg,* 2001.

Roland Flint: "Skin" and "The Green for Pamela" are from his book, *Resuming Green: Selected Poems, 1965-1982,* The Dial Press, N.Y., 1983.

Linda Nemec Foster: "Bad Art at the Clarkston Motor Inn" first appeared in *Rosebud*, 1994, and in *The Best of Rosebud,* 2001. "Nightmare" first appeared in *The Georgia Review,* 1992, and in *Living in the Fire Nest,* Ridgeway Press, 1996.

Lillian Frankel: "Dance Class" was first published in *Maryland Poetry Review,* 1994.

Sunil Freeman: "Talking" was previously published in Spring/Summer 1997 issue of *WordWrights!* and in his chapbook, *Surreal Freedom Blues,* Argonne House Press, 1999.

Martin Galvin: "The Big Leagues" was previously published in *Argestes*, 2000.

David Gewanter: "Chai 1924-2000" was first published in the on-line journal, *Slate*, 2001.

Bina Goldfield: "Stages" is from her chapbook, *Blade Against the Skin,* Singular Speech Press, 1991.

Herbert S. Guggenheim: "Pete Sussman Answers a Challenge from the Countess Lisa to Write a Sonnet in Less Than 24 Hours" first appeared in his chapbook *Pomes, Buck Each,* Ecclesiastes Press, 1994.

Daniel Gutstein: "Less and Less the Day's Happenstance" was first published in *The Midwest Quarterly.*

Jeffrey Harrison: "Our Other Sister" is from his book, *Feeding the Fire*, Sarabande Books, 2001.

Richard Harteis: "Tempus Fugit" was first published in *WPFW 89.3 Poetry Anthology,* Bunny and Crocodile Press, 1992.

Lola Haskins: "How I Learned" and "Spell for a Poet Getting On" were first published in her book, *The Rim Benders,* Anhinga, 2001.

Ava Leavell Haymon: "Four Eyes Gets Her First Warning" was first published in *The Taos Review,* 1990, and also appeared in her chapbook, *Built in Fear of Heat,* Night Shade Press, 1994.

Robert Haynes: "Peonies" was first published in *Kentucky Poetry Review,* Fall/Winter, 1989/1990.

Wendell Hawken: "Winter Scene at Evening Stables" was published in *Poet Lore,* Spring, 2001.

William Heath: "The Shining Path" was previously published in *Bells*, 1990.

Cynthia Hoffman: "Waking" was first published in *Frantic Egg,* August, 2000.

Bert Hubinger: "Nancy Reagan Looks to the East and Turns to Salt" was originally published in *Visions International, #22,* Black Buzzard Press, 1986.

Bruce A. Jacobs: "The Black Advertising Copywriter Dresses for the Theater" was first published in *Beloit Poetry Journal,* Summer, 1998.

Roy Jacobstein: "La Création" was published in *LUNA*, Summer, 2000, and "The Odd Morphology of Regret" in *Threepenny Review,* Spring, 2001.

Valerie Jean: "Thread" first appeared in the on-line journal, *Beltway*, 2000.

Rod Jellema: "Ice Age" was first published in *WordWrights!*, 1997.

Nancy Johnson: "Side Show" was first published in *Gulf Coast*, Summer, 1994.

Ann Rae Jonas: "Stroke by Stroke" was first published in her Washington Prize-winning book, *A Diamond is Hard But Not Tough*, The Word Works, 1998.

Miriam Kessler: "Beyond Belief" has been published in *Beauty for Ashes* and *Someone to Pour the Wine*, Andrew Mountain Press, 1996.

Ann B. Knox: "Circles" was first published in *Poetry*, 1992. "I Dream Old Dylan Came Back" first appeared in *Negative Capability*. Both poems also appeared in her book, *Staying is Nowhere*, SCOP Publications, 1996.

Carolyn Kreiter-Foronda: "On Monet's Studio-Boat" was first published in *Visions International*, 2001.

David Kresh: "Goodnight. Goodnight." was first published in *Chicago Review*, Winter, 1985.

Hiram Larew: An earlier version of "If He Never Hears This" appeared in *The Washington Review*, December/January, 1999/2000, and was awarded that journal's annual poetry prize.

Merrill Leffler: "Farewell" is from his book, *Take Hold*, Dryad Press, 2000.

Lenny Lianne: "Nocturne" first appeared in *Tidepools: A Journal of Ideas*, Fall, 2001.

M. L. Liebler: "A Lonely Blues to Be" first appeared in the on-line journal, *Exquisite Corpse*, Fall, 2001.

Elaine Magarrell: "Looking up from the Garden" fist appeared in the *Potomac Review*, Spring, 1998.

Sydney March: "The Summer You Said Yes to Me" is from his book, *Stealing Mangoes*, Mica Press, 1997.

David McAleavey: "February: Arlington" was first published in *Poet & Critic*.

Richard McCann: "After You Died" was published in his book, *Ghost Letters*, Alice James Books, 1994.

Judith McCombs: "Afterwards, You Learn" first appeared in *Poetry Northwest*, Winter 1998-99. Her poem, "Pictures Not in Our Albums" appeared in *Poetry Northwest*, Winter 1993-94, and in *Territories, Here and Elsewhere:* Mayapple Press, Saginaw, Michigan, 1996; 1998.

James McEuen: "The Debt" is from his book, *Snake Country*, The Word Works, 1990.

David Moolten: "Housatonic" and "Having Come This Way" are from his book, *Plums & Ashes*, Northeastern University Press, 1994.

Miles David Moore: "Duck Stamps" was published in *Buddha Isn't Laughing*, Argonne House Press, 1999 and originally appeared in *Potomac Review*, 1996, where it was that journal's annual poetry prize winner.

Kermit Moyer: "The Dream of Return" was first published in *The Cumberland Poetry Review*, Spring, 1983.

Miriam Mörsel Nathan: "Sister Maria Roberta Says the Dead Miss Us and Are Jealous" first appeared in the anthology *Daughters of Absence*, Capital Books, April, 2000.

Marie Pavlicek-Wehrli: "Song for the Trains and the Small Lost Towns" was originally published in *Firefly Magazine*, 2001.

Patric Pepper: "Fantastic Creature" is from his chapbook, *Zoned Industrial*, Medicinal Purposes, 2000.

Minnie Bruce Pratt: "The Blue Cup" was first published in her book, *Walking Back Up Depot Street*, University of Pittsburgh Press, 1999.

Mary Quattlebaum: "Cherry Tomatoes: Canning with My Sister" was first published in the *Antietam Review*, Spring, 1995.

Luis Rebaza-Soraluz: "The Keys" was translated by Elizabeth Doonan, Johnny Payne and the author. The poem was first published in *Del reino y la frontera* and *Señor Consul & Other Omnipotences*, 2001.

Elizabeth Rees: "Waiting" was previously published in *Sojourner*, November, 1990.

CABIN FEVER-

Suzanne Rhodenbaugh: "When That Sweet Wind Through My Southern Window Comes" was first published in *Barrow Street,* Fall, 1999.

Dwaine Rieves: "Aubade in E" was first published in *River Styx*, 1999.

May Rihani: "Palm Trees" was first published in her book, *...It Encircles the Waist of the Earth,* Platform International, 1993.

Hugo Rizzoli: "Putting the Aerialists to Bed" was first published in his book, *Cape Strata*, Sedwick House, 1989.

Kim Roberts: "As in a Fable" was first published in *Bibliophilos*, 2001.

Jay Rogoff: "How We Came to Stand on That Shore" is from his book, *How We Came to Stand on That Shore,* River City Publishing, 2002, and was also published in *The Quarterly,* 1991.

Robert Sargent: "Things That Go On Between Us" was first published in his book, *Aspects of a Southern Story,* The Word Works, 1983.

M. A. Schaffner: "Gutters Cleaned" was first published in *Opus*, University of Newcastle, Australia, 2001, and in *No Exit,* Winter, 2002.

Myra Shapiro: "The Wind" was first published in her book, *I'll See You Thursday,* Blue Sofa Press, 1996.

Enid Shomer: "In The Viennese Style" is from her book, *Black Drum,* University of Arkansas Press, 1997, and was first published in *Poetry*, 1991.

Myra Sklarew: "At the Syrian Border" and "Rosary" are from *Lithuania: New and Selected Poems,* Azul Editions, 1995.

J. D. Smith: "Aubade" was first published in *Erete's Bloom*, Spring, 2001.

Rose Solari: "My Mother's Piano" was first published in her book, *Selections from Myths and Elegies,* Argonne House Press, 1999.

Susan Sonde: "As Participants in a Major Production in a Classical Mode" was first published in *Potpourri*, 1999.

Gary Stein: "Subway" was first published in *Poetry*, April, 1999.

Silvana Straw: "The Acupuncturist" was first published in the *Indiana Review,* 1997.

Joseph Thackery: "In the Barn" is from his book, *The Dark Above Mad River,* Washington Writers' Publishing House, 1992.

Hilary Tham: "Standing in the dark, seeing Orion's Belt" was previously published in *Counting*, The Word Works, 2001.

Davi Walders: "Requiem for Judith Resnick" was first published in *The American Scholar*, Winter, 1997.

Charlotte Gould Warren: "Sons" was first published in *Crosscurrents*, Fall, 1999.

Michael Waters: "Parthenopi" is from his book, *Parthenopi: New and Selected Poems,* BOA Editions, 2001, and was first published in *The Georgia Review.*

Margaret Weaver: "Gravity" was first published in *Yankee Magazine,* 1999; it also appeared in her book, *Escaping Words,* Washington Writers' Publishing House, 2001.

Reed Whittemore: "The Schools" was first published in *Light, A Quarterly of Light Verse,* 1995.

Rhonda Williford: "The Witness" was first published in her book, *One Wide Sky,* Argonne House Press, 1997.

Terence Winch: "The Deal" first appeared in the magazine *Euphony*, Spring, 2001, and was included in the collection, *The Drift of Things,* The Figures, 2001.

George Young: "The Sweetness Of Disordered Air" was first published in *360 Degrees,* December, 2001.

Index by Author

CABIN FEVER--

--1984-2001

CABIN FEVER--

Index by Poem Title

---1984-2001

CABIN FEVER---

Gift Givers

Patron

Ann B. Knox

Paris Pacchione

Virginia Pauker

J.D. Smith

Anonymous

Donor

Karren Alenier

Ned Balbo

Howard Gofreed

Clarinda Harriss

Nancy Murray

Jo Radnor

Henry Taylor

Friend

John Cornelius

Dryad Press

Elizabeth Follin-Jones

Miriam Mörsel Nathan

Cynthia Turner-Graham

About The Word Works

The Word Works, a nonprofit literary organization, publishes contemporary poetry in collectors' editions. Since 1981, the organization has sponsored the Washington Prize, a $1,500 award to an American poet. Monthly, The Word Works presents free literary programs in the Chevy Chase Café Muse series, and each summer, free poetry programs are held at the historic Joaquin Miller Cabin in Washington, DC's Rock Creek Park. Annually, two high school students debut in the Miller Cabin Series as winners of the Young Poets Competition.

Since 1974, Word Works programs have included: "In the Shadow of the Capitol," a symposium and archival project on the African-American intellectual community in segregated Washington, DC; the Gunston Arts Center Poetry Series (Ai, Carolyn Forché, Stanley Kunitz, and others); the Poet-Editor panel discussions at the Bethesda Writer's Center (John Hollander, Maurice English, Anthony Hecht, Josephine Jacobsen, and others); Poet's Jam, a multi-arts program series featuring poetry in performance; a poetry workshop at the Center for Creative Non-Violence (CCNV) shelter; and the Arts Retreat in Tuscany. Master Class workshops, an ongoing program, have featured Agha Shahid Ali, Thomas Lux, and Marilyn Nelson.

In 2004, Word Works will have published 53 titles, including work from such authors as Deirdra Baldwin, J.H. Beall, Christopher Bursk, John Pauker, Edward Weismiller, and Mac Wellman. Currently, The Word Works publishes books and occasional anthologies under three imprints: the Washington Prize, the Capital Collection, and International Editions.

Past grants have been awarded by the National Endowment for the Arts, National Endowment for the Humanities, DC Commission on the Arts & Humanities, Witter Bynner Foundation, Writer's Center, Bell Atlantic, Batir Foundation, and others, including many generous private patrons.

The Word Works has established an archive of artistic and administrative materials in the Washington Writing Archive housed in the George Washington University Gelman Library.

Please enclose a self-addressed, stamped envelope with all inquiries.

The Word Works Publications

Karren L. Alenier, *Wandering on the Outside*
Karren L. Alenier, ed., *Whose Woods These Are*
Karren L. Alenier, Hilary Tham, Miles David Moore, eds., *Winners: A Retrospective of the Washington Prize*
* Nathalie F. Anderson, *Following Fred Astaire*
* Michael Atkinson, *One Hundred Children Waiting for a Train*
Mel Belin, *Flesh That Was Chrysalis* (CAPITAL COLLECTION)
* Peter Blair, *Last Heat*
Doris Brody, *Judging the Distance* (CAPITAL COLLECTION)
Christopher Bursk, ed., *Cool Fire*
Grace Cavalieri, *Pinecrest Rest Haven* (CAPITAL COLLECTION)
Christopher Conlon, *Gilbert and Garbo in Love* (CAPITAL COLLECTION)
Moshe Dor, Barbara Goldberg, Giora Leshem, eds., *The Stones Remember*
Isaac Goldberg, *Solomon Ibn Gabirol: A Bibliography of His Poems in Translation* (INTERNATIONAL EDITIONS)
* Linda Lee Harper, *Toward Desire*
James C. Hopkins, *eight pale women* (CAPITAL COLLECTION)
* Ann Rae Jonas, *A Diamond Is Hard But Not Tough*
Myong-Hee Kim, *Crow's Eye View: The Infamy of Lee Sang, Korean Poet* (INTERNATIONAL EDITIONS)
Vladimir Levchev, *Black Book of the Endangered Species* (INTERNATIONAL EDITIONS)
* Fred Marchant, *Tipping Point*
Miles David Moore, *The Bears of Paris* (CAPITAL COLLECTION)
* Jay Rogoff, *The Cutoff*
Robert Sargent, *Aspects of a Southern Story*
Robert Sargent, *A Woman From Memphis*
* Enid Shomer, *Stalking the Florida Panther*
Maria Terrone, *The Bodies We Were Loaned* (CAPITAL COLLECTION)
Hilary Tham, *Bad Names for Women* (CAPITAL COLLECTION)
Hilary Tham, *Counting* (CAPITAL COLLECTION)
* Miles Waggener, *Phoenix Suites*
* Charlotte Gould Warren, *Gandhi's Lap*
* George Young, *Spinoza's Mouse*

* *Washington Prize winners*